HOLY
SPIRIT–INSPIRED

Poetry

CAROL J. ALLEN

WESTBOW
PRESS®
A DIVISION OF THOMAS NELSON
& ZONDERVAN

WestBow Press books may be ordered through booksellers or by contacting:

WestBow Press
A Division of Thomas Nelson & Zondervan
1663 Liberty Drive
Bloomington, IN 47403
www.westbowpress.com
844-714-3454

ISBN: 978-1-6642-1736-2 (sc)
ISBN: 978-1-6642-1738-6 (hc)
ISBN: 978-1-6642-1737-9 (e)

Library of Congress Control Number: 2020925399

Print information available on the last page.

WestBow Press rev. date: 01/04/2021

Series title page

Also by Carol J. Allen: Through My Eyes

DEDICATION

This book was written for Christians, soon-to-be Christians, and those who would read this book and be encouraged to become Christians.

Acknowledgments

I give thanks to the following people who were instrumental in the encouragement of this book.

My husband, William H. Allen, who put all the poems on the computer for the transmission. Pastor Al Cabrera for his encouragement. And William H. Stickney Jr. for editing the manuscript.

INTRODUCTION

This book contains much of the poetry written to accompany the weekly sermons at Willow River Baptist Church of Houston under Pastor Al Cabrera. It contains poems written over several years. Pastor Cabrera gave me the sermon scriptures each week to write a related poem to print in the bulletin. Many poems came to me in the middle of the night, and I would quickly rise to put them on paper. Only the Holy Spirit could allow me the words to write.

CONTENTS

A Change of Ways

Being a sinner of great remorse,
I strive for righteousness as a new course.
Just as being slovenly will not bring the good life,
No one attains heaven with sin and strife.

With the Holy Spirit keeping one in tow,
How difficult can it be for the good side to show?
Focus on Jesus and what He would do;
Abandon your sins like a dirty old shoe.

Pray and praise for focus anew,
Then before you know it your time is filled,
And sin has been discarded behind the last hill.

A Child of God

Lord, You didn't give me beauty,
But You gave what was best.
Then, Lord, You put me to the test.

I don't have riches, but I do have wealth
For I have the Holy Spirit inside myself.
I pray that I'll deliver
All You planned for me to do.

So day by day I'll become
A little more like You.

A Helping Hand

Once I was like a sheep,
Lost and nothing went right.
How could I have gone astray?
Why, oh why, had I acted that way?

Then I prayed to the Lord.
The Lord's light came shining through
As He sent my salvation
In the person of You.

Reaching out, He lifted me up,
Took away the pain,
And filled my cup.

And so I say for all to hear
He'll do the same for those
Who dare to draw Him near.

A King Is Born

In love He lived,
Humble and giving,
Touching and healing,
Ever forgiving.

The perfect example of all we should be.
Then He was crucified, yet you can see
He forgave the likes of you and me.

Each year we celebrate His birth
As He alone has given us worth.
I bend my knee and praise His name,
And have eternal gratitude because He came.

Inspiration from
Luke 2:1–13

A King Was Born

A king was born to show the way.
In humble form He came to save the day.

A king suffered and died then rose again
To stem the evil that plagued all men.

In His place He sent a comforter
To dwell in every Christian supporter.

We celebrate His birth
And all His time on earth.

Happy birthday, baby Jesus.
We give thanks for all Your work.

A MISSION TO THE PHILIPPINES

Two thousand was God's approved time
For a mission trip to the Philippines, I find.
We dyed our hair black that we might blend in,
Something like our black-haired, dark-skinned friends.
But our hair remained light, and our skin was too white.
God said, "You'll accomplish more by far
If you go as you are."

We traveled through Manila, Zamboanga, and Cebu
With our Philippine friend, and then we traveled home again.
He had opened the door and guided us each day.

Our mission was accomplished, and we did it God's way.

Also published in my first book, *Through My Eyes*, AuthorHouse, 2008, page 31.

A MOTHER

The rock upon which a family thrives,
The binding for which all are linked and survive.
A virtual servant to man and child,
"Loving" and "caring" are words too mild.

With power and love equally on display,
She rises and ends each strenuous day,
Taking care of and nurturing all who came her way.

Living by example with that awesome smile,
Like a magnet she draws you to stay for a while
She'll sing you a song and caress your hurts,
And always accompany her husband and child to church.

A New Life (Born Again)

Here is how my life did begin—
Lots of crying and filled with sin.
In growing up, sin was in.

Pain and sorrow took hold;
Devastation began to unfold.
Then one day a friend picked me up.
He said, "My church will fill your cup."

There I dropped to my knees.
He took my hand and gave it a squeeze.
After repeating what he said to me,
Something had changed; I could see.
Suddenly words came out of me.

Words I didn't understand,
Yet this is where it all began.
I felt clean and filled with grace,
Sensing the Holy Spirit had settled into place.

He revealed things I never knew
And leads my life in all I do.
He became my comforter, leader, and friend.
He talks to me and walks with me again and again.

He has opened every door
And changed my life forever more.
He turns the lights on both day and night,
And raises my spirits to joy and delight.

There isn't anything I cannot do
For He directed my life anew.
That's how I know I am born again,
Seeing His works a lot, not just now and then.

A New Year

A year has come and is about to go.
One thing to be sure of, and wisely so, is
That we can do better wherever we go.

A renewing of the mind, a better way,
A different focus—God's work put in play.

Jesus leads, this is true.
But if we're not listening, what will we do?
Will we do it our way or His?
Will we succeed, or will we fizzle and fizz?

Let the Holy Spirit be your guide.
Search deep down inside.
Let that still small voice override.
Focus on Him, and set your ways aside.

For God knows all your desires and needs,
Which He'll satisfy as His will succeeds.

A New Year Begins

A new year begins.
What will unfold?
Within the Bible our future is told.

What is our part to do
As we witness the prophecies come true?
Will we be able to show our love
And still be brave and in one accord?

While the enemy boldly waves its sword
As if denouncing our Savior and Lord?

Will our faith in the Lord stand strong
Or fear of the sword make us choose wrong?
In Christ, remember who you are
For our rewards will be better by far.

A PURPOSE-FILLED LIFE

All are born with a purpose in mind.
A plan to follow Jesus, we'll find.

To continue His work day after day,
Following His lead and doing it His way.

And we will be protected till our work is done,
Then we will reap our rewards with Father and Son.

Sickness and pain are but for a day,
And all will end in a wonderful way!

Inspiration from
Acts 28:1–10

A Song of Love

Lord of Lords,
King of Kings,
Giver of life
And of all things.

Let me be generous
With all my gifts,
Sprinkling them with wisdom
For a life to lift.

Still the waters
That I go through.
Show me the path
That leads straight to You.

A Sunny Day

Wake up in the morning and begin to pray.
And what do you have in mind, Lord, for me today?

All around it pours down rain;
Slow-moving traffic and danger abide.
Yet it nourishes the land to our gain
And reminds me of how pleasant it will soon be inside.

Nothing too eventful gets under way.
Problems arise, and for solutions we pray.
All in all, a very good day.

Driving home and the sun is out.
"Praise the Lord!" erupts in a shout.

For all the good thoughts stay
And the bad have all passed away.

A Time to Speak

Here is how we do things God's way,
A way to put His Word in to play.
The time and place and what you say,
Guided by the Holy Spirit will show the way.

Wisdom and courage come in play
When your words impact this day.
Don't let them fall on barren ground,
But speak to the lost and needy all around.

Wisdom on what to say
To those of leadership could save the day.
Help your brothers who have gone astray,
Enthusiastically doing all in the Lord's way.

Inspiration from
Acts 25:1–12

ACTION, NOT WORDS

Anyone spoiling for a fight
Won't find one in my sight.
Confrontation goes in one ear and out the other;
I learned how to do that with my sisters and brothers.

Distracting them helped a lot,
By showing my love right on the spot.
Cupping their faces gently with my hands.
I'm not the enemy but one of the fans.

Letting them know that even though we might not agree,
We have binds that tie, yet we are also free.
I'd rather show them the best of me,
Not just for them, but for all to see.

ADVERSITY

Evil, like a disease,
Is growing rapidly and with ease.
Yet we continue to struggle

To spread God's Word,
Bravely pushing forward to be heard.

No time for fear or doubt,
The Lord's Word must be heard throughout.

Spread it everywhere you can.
Live it and take your stand.

ALL GOD'S CHILDREN

My eyes heed no color or race,
No religion or specific place.

For we were made equal in spirit,
And we must make sure that the
Word is spread for everyone to hear it.

Sharing your home, food, and drink
Forms a bond that will help God's family grow.

We venture forward to seek
Even those whom we don't yet know.

ALL THINGS NEW

God made all things from beginning to end.
And fashioned after Him were the likes of men.
He predetermined the life of all,
Setting the time for His creations to rise and fall.

The birth and death of all living things
Are in His hands and under His wing.

What you do with His precious gifts
Will bring you down or enhance and lift.
Be vigilant for the time grows near
When all will be gone, and new will appear.

Inspiration from
Ecclesiastes 3:11;
Revelation 21:5.

Another Year

Everything has a beginning on this earth;
Everything has an end after showing worth.
Another year has come and gone
In which you have done both right and wrong.

This is a time to review your past,
A time to reflect on what would last.
Renew your vows with your Father God, and
Listen for the Holy Spirit's prodding.

Make changes and peace along the way,
Reflecting from day to day.
You never know when you'll be called home,
So smile, sing, and make a tone.

ARE YOU READY?

Standing in the midst of corruption and despair
Are the Christians gathering from here and there.
You can tell by their reverence to God,
With their hands held high and knees bent,
Gathered together in humble assent.

Woe to those who do not heed
The Bible signs that we foresee.
Like Sodom and Gomorrah, He'll take all out,
The leaders of evil and all that follow.

The days are numbered, so make haste;
There is no time to waste.
Yesterday, today, and tomorrow won't delay.
Today is the time to mend any sinful thought or sinful way.

As You Sow

If someone does you wrong
And you reciprocate,
Or if you give in love
To someone who doesn't appreciate;

Here's a thought to ponder.
What you sow you'll also reap.
Don't act like your enemy.
Remember, Jesus died for you and me
When all us sinners wouldn't set Him free.

That's the way we need to be.
Our greatest reward is heaven.
Have faith and you will see.

ATTITUDE

Keep in your heart an attitude of gratitude.
Let nothing else creep in
For the heart is the part that keeps
The rest of you from sin.

If the head overpowers the heart,
Then sin and pride will be its mark.
You're never too old to be God's child,
And He knows how to tame a child gone wild.

Boast of the Lord Jesus, Holy Spirit, and God above.
For then you'll remember the greatest gift is love.

Babble or Bible?

How do we discern self-proclaimed babble?
We check the verification in the Bible.
Those who spread myths from they know not where,
Could not have checked the Bible before they cared to share.

Not to be mistaken for experiences they knew,
But even those are examples of what God will do.
So stay in tune with the Holy Spirit, and read your Bible,
And then better you'll discern all that is worthwhile.

BAPTISM

Baptism, baptism, what can one say?
Outwardly, a dedication to God on display,
A family affair put in to play.

Yet being born again is clearly a must.
Easily done without fanfare or fuss,
A pledge of the heart from each of us.

Inspiration from
Acts 16:30–34.

BEAUTY

God made the universe and all that's in it.
Yes, even the earth, a world of plenty and worth.

Then He made us in His image so great,
Even making both male and female to fill our plate.
As He formed a union with all that is alive
Ensuring all would survive.

Yet like angry children we've gone astray,
Abusing God's gifts along the way,
Trampling our brothers without regard.
For this I pray and weep so hard.

Forgive them Father, for they know not what they do.
Help us all to change their focus to be more like You.

Inspiration from
Genesis 1–31;
Hebrews 11:10.

BEGINNING OF SORROWS

The day of sorrow will be the completed task
Before vindication will come at last.
Yet after the sorrow follows the tribulation
Engulfing the world, nation upon nation.

The sun and moon will show no light.
The stars will fall and the powers of heaven shake,
Revealing in the clouds the Son of man we await.
Trumpets will sound and the gathering of the elect.

So do not fret if it is not over yet.
Prepare and believe through wars, famine,
Money, pestilence, earthquakes, and false gods
For the seals must be opened before tribulation and God.

BEHIND THE POWER

Lawmakers may grow out of control,
But God sends a consequence, as we all know.
Among His people are the chosen ones.
Heed the warning for His will shall be done.

Sing out, you soldiers, emanate His voice!
God's in control and knows your choice.
You are the mouthpiece, and God will do the rest.
Faith in the Lord is what we know best.

BEHOLD SUCH BEAUTY

First came the beauty of the universe.
Then came the beauty in it.
To finish, He made man for a perfect fit.

His artistry unmatched,
He gathered the beauty from His earth
And formed our lives of great worth.
Each uniquely different from the other;
Each put together, entwined by a father and mother.

Like an artist using many shades and color,
Yet arms, legs, bodies, and heads make us sister and brother.
Fashioned like Him, we are like no other.

God is one in Father, Son, and Holy Spirit.
And we, too, are one in body, soul, and spirit.

Believe

Pain and sorrow in any day
Can bring you closer to the Lord.
Or it can take you further away.
Here is what I have to say.

Those who trust in Him
Will find Him near.
And those who do not talk to Him
Will find Him quite hard to hear.

The Lord suffered for us,
Which we constantly discuss.

But let's talk about today
As we suffer for Him in a much milder way.
For He, too, knows our path each day
And promises great rewards in a beautiful way.

Inspiration from
Psalm 34:18;
Romans 8:18.

BELIEVE, LOVE, OBEY

Jesus paid the price to open the door
That we could be kings and priests evermore.
Faith in God and who you are is critical by far.
If you are in need, ask the Lord and believe to succeed.

Don't pray for healing then declare you are sick.
For the Lord will give you what you confess real quick.
Don't confess your sins and think that's all you need do
For He knows your heart and if your confession is true.

Obeying God's will is what you strive to do.
Even when you slip and slide, God's love comes through.

Speaking of love, as you well know, it is clearly told
Love is more precious than silver and gold.
For you are commanded to love your brother as yourself.
Without love, in vain is everything else.

Inspiration from
1 John 5:6–12.

BIBLE MESSAGES

It has been my experience every day
That poetry and the Bible are the same way.
Some poetry verses are for you, not me;
Bible passages are not necessarily for all to see.

I've read a passage over and over again,
And maybe someday I will understand.
The Lord would say be rest assured,
All you need to know is in My Word.

What you don't understand is not for you.
Yet there is something you can do.
Go to the One who has been designated to say
How the Bible is put in play.

Inspiration from
Acts 8:30–40.

BORN AGAIN

I have the Lord in my life, oh yes!
I have the Lord in my life.
I praise Him every day in all that I say.
I have the Lord in my life!

I have His song in my heart, oh yes!
I have His song in my heart,
And I'll sing of Him every day.
Forever, come what may.

For I have His song in my heart.
Sing praises to His name,
And rise to the glory of His light.

Sing praises of His greatness
As you sleep in His peace tonight.

Also published in my first book, *Through My Eyes*, AuthorHouse, 2008, page 12.

BUILDING YOUR CROWN

The believing or unbelieving Jew or
The gentile, which is me and you,
Either throws stones at the likes of Paul,
Or joins the works of the apostles,
Teaching the Word to all.

Praying and healing and showing the way,
Regardless of the consequences each and every day.

As the devil tries to stop you anyway he can,
You tire, fall, become discouraged, and then
Pick yourself up and start again!

Remember this to be true,
That heaven awaits to reward all that you do.

BUSY, BUSY

Up in the morning,
Out on the job.
No time to waste,
No time to hobnob.

First work on the job
Then errands to run.
Supper to make,
House to clean.
Every day the same routine.

Head for the bed,
Turn down the phone.
It can be thankfully said
Hurrah for any time of my own!

Also published in my first book, *Through My Eyes*, AuthorHouse, 2008, page 28.

CELEBRATE

The pine tree all aglow;
The lights glitter to present a show.
Gifts of love begin to flow,
Yet this is what I feel and know.

Equal parts of happy and sad—
Partly sorrow, partly glad—
Knowing we celebrate Jesus's birth
For His short time on this earth

To free us from our sin
And let the Holy Spirit in.
Born humble and died in pain
Just so we could be adopted in His name.

Happy birthday, Jesus.

CELEBRATE, CELEBRATE

So you wanna get married.
Family and friends are here to celebrate.
Even though it's a little scary,
We know you just can't wait.

We're gonna celebrate, celebrate!

Take with you the Father, Son, and Holy Ghost
For their presence will help the most.
Knowing all of this, father sits silently,
And mother cries for all to see.

Still we're gonna celebrate, celebrate!

Nowhere else can you find more joy and love
Than in the perfect mate picked from heaven above.

So you're gonna get married.
Let's all celebrate, celebrate!

CHARACTER OF GOD

Paul and Barnabas, missionaries together,
Did dispute, separate to spread wide and better.
Today with me and you, godly characteristics.
Is the Holy Ghost coming through?

Gentle traits, like a child on Daddy's knee,
Nurturing with love and planting a seed.
Putting food in a hungry mouth,
Lifting one up who is down and out.

Mercy and compassion can be found
Helping on the misfortunes of others around.
These characteristics found in dying to self,
Being born again so the Holy Spirit can help,
While getting power and strength in the fight
Against sin throughout your life.

CHILD TO FATHER

Lord, you know our hearts and minds.
There is no sin that can be hid of any kind.
You gave us the Holy Spirit to help,
Yet our weakness to sin can still be felt.

Like my mother always said,
"I abhor your sin but love you instead."

He already knows our sin.
Pray for forgiveness for the healing to begin.
Not like a ritual coming from our head
But love of a child for his Father instead.

Inspiration from
Hebrews 4:14–16.

Children of
Disobedience

Disobedience runs rampant over the land.
Fear and heartbreak close at hand.
No one seems concerned, and none understand.
These are our leaders of tomorrow:
Self-willed and cruel predict pain and sorrow.

Who cares if Mother is being abused,
Or Dad would kill before he would lose.
Who cares if baby watches the scene,
And as he grows up repeats what he's seen.

Spoil the child; let him do what he wants.
Disrespect is acceptable as seen every day.
Question a parent, and this they will say,
"We can't discipline them, and there's no other way!"

How did we get in such a state?
Do you think there's a chance, or is it too late
To change what is happening, to cause such a fate?
And having one parent is definitely not great.

Feuding and fighting are part of it all.
Killing for religion, an excuse to brawl.
Discarding each other when newness wears off
Helps teach little children it's not necessary to bond.
So pain and sorrow march on.

Also published in my first book, *Through My Eyes*, AuthorHouse, 2008, page 39.

Children of Obedience

Born in sin yet conceived in love,
Chosen parents both on earth and heaven above.
For each, God has a plan.
But if you don't follow it, grief is at hand.

For the devil entices with many "good" things.
To serve God doesn't always bring diamonds and rings.
God's rewards are subtle and sweet,
A roof over your head and something to eat.

Not things you buy at the store
But peace, love, healing, and so much more.
Heaven or hell, which will you choose?
Make a decision now for there's no time to lose!

Disobeying parents is disobeying God,
And both may discipline with an iron rod.

Inspiration from
John 8:32–44.

CHOSEN

Short is the path of birth to death;
This we cannot forget.
Part of that time is growing up,
Learning and seeking to fill our cup.

At the age the Lord has designed,
We become aware and slowly find
That childhood is left behind,
And how to serve God enters our mind.

Do not be afraid for you will know
God will provide your way to go.
So open your mouth and live His style
For all the rewards waiting past this trial.

Inspiration from
Acts 26:12–23.

CHRISTIAN FATHERS

Christian fathers should never desert,
To leave their families desolate and hurt.
To do this they stand center and front.
The leaders of power, to be blunt.

Humble before their family,
Yet wise and brave against any enemy.
Setting an example from day to day
At work, at home, at play.

Always respecting family and friends,
But equally the like unto all men.
May God influence and bless,
Surrounding them like a wind's caress.

Inspiration from
Deuteronomy 6:6–9.

CHRISTIANITY

The Bible teaches our history,
Our present, and the future.
Yet back when Jesus came to earth
To take away sin and give us worth,

How great it must have been
To reach and touch Him
As He walked among men.

To see Him work undeterred,
To listen to His every word.
Yet I see His work every day
And sense His presence in every way.

CHRISTLIKE

My desire, Lord, is to be more like You
In everything I say and in everything I do.
Never giving in to sin and evil,
Always fighting off the devil.

We are the Lord's army, I'd say.
And the Holy Spirit leads the way.
If I suffer pain and sorrow for Your will,
My heart will show I love You still.

And if You should bless my way,
I'll share it with others every day.

Nothing I could suffer through
Could ever compare to what You do.
For this I know, Your love will see me through.

Clean Inside and Out

We are sinners in a world filled with sinners.
Yet in all of this, we are still winners.
For we have fellowship with Jesus Christ Himself,
Intimately confiding and confessing our imperfect self.

As He is forgiving for each imperfect day,
Sending us out cleansed in His way.

Sounds much like taking a morning shower,
Then slowly getting dirty hour by hour.
Just to wake the next morning to another shower.
Oh, thank You, Jesus, knowing Your love receives us.

Inspiration from
1 John 1–5:10.

COMING UP

The ship is sinking, as you know.
God will be choosing where each shall go.

Will you be chosen to rise and meet Him?
Or will you remain to begin again.
Will you be ready for His call?
Do you even think about it at all?

Now is the time to show you care.
Now is the time to prepare.
Now is the time to pave the way
For whatever God chooses for us that day.

COMMITMENT

Here I drove down the road
When the Lord descended upon my soul.

The car music played a Christian song,
And I began to sing along.

He said, "It is time for you to follow me.
Friend or enemy, all must see.

The way will not be easy or fair,
But much will be accomplished for I am there."

Yes, this is what the Lord said to me.
So I embrace to be what must be,
And praise the Lord for all to see.

Inspiration from
Acts 24:22–27.

DAY AND NIGHT

Two children conceived in love,
Both are gifts from above.
We'll call one "Day" and the other one "Night".
Being different was part of the plight.

Night was difficult, turning life upside down.
While Day was a delight just being around.

Over the years, lots of direction turned Night into Day.
But lack of attention turned Day the other way.
Which way to go? What to do?
Let's hope this doesn't happen to you.

Dealing with Sin

Meet the misguided where they are.
Teach them the rewards beyond the evil bar.
Jesus came to seek out the lost.
He did it very well, knowing the cost.

Our job is to take the Word to all who will listen.
Showing the good against evil is our mission.
If we love our neighbor and they love us back,
We have our reward and are right on track.

But if we take the Word to the lost
And they do not agree,
Don't take them home, but let them be.
For there are so many we have yet to see.
Praise to the Lord from you and me.

Inspiration from
Luke 19:1–10.

DEATH OF A LADY

On a porch in a rocker sits a lady.
She is old, and her hair has turned to gray.
She just sits all alone in that rocker
And slowly gently rocks her life away.

Doesn't anybody care about this lady?
Doesn't anybody want to know?
Where are the children of her youth?
Where did all her loved ones go?

Look at the smile on her face.
See the tears in her eyes.
Down within, the flames burn low.
I think this lady will die.

See the sunset in the west.
A blanket of darkness o'er her pressed.
And with the darkness the flame went out.

It must have been the hand of God
That came to take her home.
He took her there to be with Him.
Now she'll never be alone.

Also published in my first book, *Through My Eyes*, AuthorHouse, 2008, page 35.

Collected Whispers, International Library of Poetry, 2008.

DECEPTION

The devil knows the Bible as
Much as or more than you or me.

The devil may take it out of
Context or change a word or two

In an attempt to deceive the
Likes of me or you.

Interpreting those precious
Words from good to evil is his forte.

He'll make it seem so logical
In what he'll say.

If you're born again, search
Your soul and pray.

Ask God's interpretation,
Then do all things His way!

DESTINY

The audacity of man
To strive for fortune and fame throughout the land,
Not receiving God's blessing or hand.

That's set the world in chaos and confusion,
A consequence of their egotistic delusion.

If you think you can do it all by yourself,
Drop to your knees, repent, and experience God's wealth.
For the door to heaven does not open wide,
And God will select who goes inside.

DEVOTION

God has given us a way
To show our devotion from day to day,
In spite of the evil that lurks all around,
Rising and falling in a world upside down.

He gave us all a choice and set in us His voice,
Gave us a plan and a choice.

If we are willing to die for a stranger, friend, or child,
Put on blinders for only a one-mate style.
Then our character is already there
To stand for God no matter what or where.

Inspiration from
Joshua 24:15;
Matthew 5:37.

DISRESPECT

First, God gave us a garden.
And we abused it.
He then gives us the earth,
Sufficient for us to use it.

To love and think for ourselves.
Yet a book of guidance lies on our shelf.
All of these things we proceeded to waste,
Destroying all with fanfare and haste.

So God sent His Son to pay for our sin.
Even with this sacrifice, many won't give in.
Now we have disasters of great magnitude,
As well as disasters we make, so callous and rude.

But every time we get a new start,
Too many join hands and tear it apart.
I'm so glad to be saved by the grace of God,
Never to be poked by the devil's rod.

Also published in *Who's Who in American Poetry 2017*, Eber & Wein
Publishing's, 2018.

DREAMS CAN COME TRUE

Just like Joseph, we all have dreams.
But most fall apart at the seams.
With God's blessing, an action speaks louder than a word,
Yet envy follows success often to be heard.

One doesn't need to boast or brag,
But teach others who tend to lag.
True wealth comes from love and giving
As the Lord smiles and enhances your living.

Always remember God rights all wrongs.
So under all circumstances, rejoice with prayer and songs.

EASY PREY

Brother, sister, relative, or child of woe,
Mother, father, friend, or foe.
So complacent, void of conscience, wanders to and fro,
Hurting others as they go.

Dealt with by God's Word, the Bible does show,
Adam or Cain and others of fame.
Today the same known by any other name,
Still, as sinners, we cannot condemn.

For final judgment is not by men,
And for unforgiveness, we cease to foresee
The children of God we were meant to be.
If God can forgive, why can't we?

ENTER JESUS

God gave this land to Adam and Eve,
But the devil did beguile and deceive.
Now chaos spreads throughout the land,
The devil's work in huge command.

But then Jesus says that for those who believe in Him,
He will return, their life to retrieve,
And the reign of Satan to fall under His feet.

The followers of evil to end and in exile be.
Those who hurt Israel will suffer the more,
And those who embrace her will be redeemed for sure.

ETHICS

There are consequences for all we do.
Sometimes good, sometimes bad, it's true.
Especially with a child being raised in the Lord's style,
Show by example is a good start, but not just for a while.

To add rules and enforce them are valuable tools.
Adults follow examples today and tomorrow.
Breaking the laws of God and man
Has consequences in heaven and on this land,
Affecting those who by your side stand.

Teach love and compassion and care
For all the rewards we might share.

Inspiration from
Luke 16:31;
Colossians 4.

Ever Changing

Lord, You know me from beginning to end.
You know my thoughts and move my pen.

Surrounded by Your children, just like me,
Whose sins are bared for all to see.

We pray Your forgiveness and correct our wrongs,
Gathering together in these coming days.

Humble before God and man, we sing songs of praise
And renew our pledge to change our ways.

Inspiration from
Proverbs 28:13;
2 Corinthians 5:10.

FAITH

In an imperfect world of folks
Mingles a most perfect host.
Faith in Him brings perseverance galore.
Faith in Him, whether rich or poor,
Faith in the will and ways of the Lord.

All that is earthly withers in age.
We were not promised riches or fame.
But like Jesus on earth, some sorrow and pain,
We may suffer today, but in His arms, tomorrow,
Imperfections gone with pain and sorrow.

Faith and the Holy Spirit

The Holy Spirit speaks.
Into the heart and mind He seeps.
In a language only you can know,
To resonate in the ways we go.

The devil cannot penetrate,
Only react to our actions and faith.
The more we have faith to believe,
The more in life we will succeed.

The more the devil interferes,
The more the Holy Spirit must be here
To quell our weaknesses and our fear.

Inspiration from
Acts 11:8–18.

Faith Brings Understanding

All the joy the Lord has for you
Will never ever come true
If jealousy, ego, and pride rule,
Like a rebellious child skipping school.

The Lord will teach and be your guide
If you humbly open your heart to let Him inside.
And oh, the wonders that will unfold,
When upon you His glory begins to take hold.

Inspiration from
Acts 13:44–52.

FAITH IN PLACE

God is never early and never late.
When disaster looms, one must wait.

For He will respond at the right time.
If you can hear Him, get in line.

Like a football player when the ball is thrown,
Must be in place to take it on home.

Listen to God every day.
See what He is putting in play.

Before you know it, your problem soon goes away.

Inspiration from
Acts 27:18–26.

FAITH POWER

Help to a person in need
Is material but helpful indeed.
Yet the best thing you can do
Is let your faith come shining through.

It's true the Lord can do anything;
Asking in faith is what results bring.
You may ask till the cows come home,
But without faith, prayer won't unfold.

We all have the body from which the Lord works,
But faith is the connection necessary to insert.
The interaction that makes all things work?
Let's lift up one another, sister and brother.

Inspiration from
Acts 3:1–10.

FAITH-FILLED ATTITUDE

Jesus is with you in good times and bad,
Poor or rich, happy or sad.
He does not respond to fortune and fame
But the size of your faith and how you honor His name.

Follow His ways, and riches will come.
Not necessarily silver and gold,
But contentment and joy as you grow old.

If your prayers do not seem to be heard,
Have faith; watch as He makes good in His Word.
The way it may come could be a surprise
For the Lord knows what's best in His eyes.

Inspiration from
James 1:1–11.

FAT CITY

All of my life I've been skinny,
Skinny as a pin.
Then when I turned fifty,
Fat came pouring in.

No matter how I diet or how much I do not eat,
Fat plagues my belly, arms, legs, and seat.

I don't need an enemy from the North, East, West, or South.
My enemy is fat, and I just can't get fat out.

It gathers everywhere inside and shows on every inch of hide.
So everyone in the world can see
What clothes can't even hide.

Also published in my first book, *Through My Eyes*, AuthorHouse, 2008, page 26.

FATHER AND SONS

Our heavenly Father sends His sons onto the land
To raise His children as best they can.

And when that chore is done,
The Father calls home His son.

How bittersweet comes that day
When Father greets son
And we must stay.

Father, Father

Fathers of yesterday,
The family foundation paved the way.

Where are so many fathers of today?
If we could find them,
What would they say?

What will happen tomorrow,
When bonding and love are replaced by sorrow?

Let not your heart grow cold,
So a family of love will surround you
As you grow old.

Let the love of God never grow cold
But be displayed in His image, like fathers of old.

Inspiration from
1 Timothy 1:2;
Philemon 8–10.

FATHERS

The seed qualifies as a father,
But one must be special to be a dad.
From generation to generation, it is so sad
To see so many fathers and so few dads.

God placed humanity in the seed of men.
Man seeks the right woman to minister, and then
He leads by example from beginning to end
How to live for God with principles and morals alike,
Determining always what's wrong and what's right.

Fighting Sin

Sin creeps in like a thief in the night,
Not to be seen, yes, out of sight.
It robs you of morals with a different point of view.
So let me tell you what to do.

Sing God's praises morning, noon, and night.
Learn His Word and His delight.
Talk to Him, and pray with all your might.
Have faith that He will direct your plight.

When those who cry out in dismal despair,
Have sympathy and care.
But don't jump in and add to stress.
Point to the direction you think best.

You can hold their hand,
But they must decide and take a stand.

Inspiration from
Psalm 1:1–3.

FOLLOW JESUS

Hello brother, hello sister, let's break bread.
Let's not hassle but talk life and love instead.
Let's walk together; let's talk together and work things out.
Then join together and tell the world with a shout.

Let's do as Jesus did when He was here,
Being humble yet strong without fear.
He ate with us, healed, and taught.
Now we can join Him in heaven as we ought.

Let's walk this earth together,
Braving the storms of life and weather.
With the Holy Spirit, how can we miss
Spreading the gospel to live in bliss?

Inspiration from
Isaiah 1:18; John 21:12.

Follow Jesus, Please

A fight takes two.
Let's not make it me and you.
It's said a rotten apple spoils the barrel,
But will love do the same?
Well let's try and make it our aim.

The Holy Spirit is within.
Listening for Him will help you win.
Wake each morning
With a bright, sunny smile.
Vow to use it with wisdom and style.

Be honest and encouraging.
And in all things be true,
Realizing others are affected by
What you say and do.

Inspiration from
Ephesians 4:1–3.

FOR A SEASON

Many people will pass through your life.
Some will bring happiness, some strife.

They are there but for a season.
God has placed them for a reason.

Each bears a lesson God will teach
To complete the goal He wants you to reach.

Inspiration from
Isaiah 8:2;
2 Timothy 2:2.

FORGET NOTS

I can remember to pay the bills
But not where I put them, if you will.
And I can remember to make an appointment
But not the date or where it went.

My drawers are filled with pills of all kinds.
But what they are for is not written, I find.
And my bookshelf is empty due to books loaned out.
To whom they were loaned, I can't figure out.

My mother had said to make a note to help.
But inadvertently I threw the note out.
Here a note, there a note, everywhere a note.
Now which one and where is the right one I wrote?

I'll call a friend with something to say.
But first, to be polite, I'll let her talk away.
Then she'll ask, "And why did you call?"
I'll have forgotten, so the answer is, "No reason at all."

"Put it on a bulletin board," you say.
Then what do I do when I'm away?
Tell me, tell me what would you do?
Hurry to answer; that is if you can find me to.

Also published in my first book, *Through My Eyes*, AuthorHouse, 2008, page 44.

From the Beginning

God spoke, and all came to be—
The sky, the earth, flowers, and trees.
Not just the world but you and me,
And the big, big sea.

But because of sin, our life was dim.
Until He sent Jesus, our redeeming light,
And the chance by adoption to become right.
You could feel—and see—His light.

But John the Baptist to lead the way,
Preaching and baptizing from day to day.
Sent to spread the good news
With special insight, never to lose.

FRUIT

We are like fruit on the tree,
At first just as green as we can be.
Then as we ripen and mature,
We show the best the Holy Spirit does procure.

Storms in life cannot stop our course
As we give our best with vigor and force.
All that wisdom and knowledge profound,
If we are not absorbed, falls to the ground.

A place where life began
To yield new fruit all over again.

Inspiration from
1 Corinthians 13:9–12.

GENEROSITY

Holy Spirit, You've called on me
To begin a generosity spree.
Now just how do You want me to start?
You want me to open my pockets and heart!

Give my time, goods, and joy, You say.
Share with all in need today.
"Never mind, You say, "for what you give.
It will be replenished as long as you live."

The Lord will direct my aim.
Just tell everyone from whence it came.
This will show my thanks for all He's done,
Abundant praise to the Holy One.

GET BEHIND ME, DEVIL

The devil made me do it is just an excuse
To live one's life wild and loose.

The devil looks for whom he may devour,
Tantalizes and urges, hour after hour.
All things present, two ways to go,
God's way or the devil's, as you should know.

The choice is yours—for instant gratification
Or for eventual long-term blessed manifestation.
The road to heaven is difficult, no doubt.
But not more than Jesus went through to give you an out.

Things of this earth are only for a while.
And it will mean nothing when you walk that last mile.

Inspiration from
Matthew 4:1–11.

GIFTS

The Lord has given His children many gifts.
Each gift has the purpose for Jesus to lift.

Others may look at you in wonder.
But don't let ego and pride drive you asunder.

Be humble, and use the gifts for His glory.
Sing His praises, and spread His story.

GIFTS OF TALENT

Born with a purpose and a plan,
The gifts God has given are easily at hand.
His pleasure and your pleasure coincide
When His gifts are used and not set aside.

Each talent given to expand and share,
Enhancing others' lives with loving care.

Not building riches or fame for your name,
But pleasing our Lord from whence it came.
Fulfilling His purpose is your aim.

Inspiration from
Mark 8:36;
1 Corinthians 10:31.

GIVING

I give to you, and you give to me,
A circle of love for all to see.
The more infectious it becomes,
The more God is pleased
That we should plant His gifts like seeds.

And in His everlasting love, it's seen
That God reciprocates by fulfilling every dream,
Whether it be health, wealth, or anything in between.

Of course He leads the way,
Showing us the gift of love each and every day.

GLORY AND THE FIRE

Before
"What is that?" you say.
"Am I saved?" you ask.
Glory and the Fire will show the way!
"Will you come and see?" you ask.
I'll just see if
Glory and the fire can convince someone like me.

After
I feel something in this place.
I must hurry to be saved in all due haste.
Lord, I didn't know the way to go
Until I saw this revealing show.
This is real; how filled I feel.
Tell me, Lord, what is Your will?

Also published in my first book, *Through My Eyes,* AuthorHouse, 2008, page 5.

GOD ALSO CHOSE ME

Lord, I know not how or why, when, or where.
Many questions I'd like to share.

Yet I accept what You ask of me,
And happily, thank You on bended knee
That You would choose someone like me.

However unworthy I might be,
My body a host to the Holy Ghost.

Yet He doesn't use me like a puppet
For I am adopted, and I love it.

Me, His child, yielding to His will,
The plan He has for me to fulfill.

GOD AND ME

Before you stands a child of God.
Steadfast on this soil I trod.
My Father died that I might live.
Then He entered heaven to make a
Place that I might live.

He sent a Comforter to help my way
So that I should not go astray.
He's with me day and night,
Wakes with me in the morning
And is there when I turn off the light.

His Word is my command,
And on this ground will firmly stand.
The love between us will never die
For He lives within, whether I laugh or cry.

Inspiration from
Psalm 119:9–16.

GOD CHOSE YOU

The Lord operates through man,
Chosen and verified by miracles at hand.
Their identity cannot be missed
For the accuracy and power are not at risk.

The promises of God will come alive
Through the Lord or through man.
His Word, as written, will survive.

Listen to the Holy Spirit, who guides today.
As to right or wrong, He'll lead the way.
Perception of a Christian put in play.

GOD OR MAN

The commands of God and man
Must be kept as best you can.

But what if they collide?
Then seek the Holy Spirit as your guide.

Remember God has placed you with a plan
Then sent you forward in this land.

Life here is like a journal.
But life with God springs eternal.

Inspiration from
Acts 5:25–32.

GOD THE FATHER'S DESIRE

Talk to your Father all day long
With prayer, repentance, and a song.

He knows what you want.
He knows what you need.
But if you don't ask,
Desires and needs may go to seed.

He sacrificed His Son just for you.
He wants the same loyalty to come through.
A bond that none can break
Will surely ensure you get through the gate.

Inspiration from
Matthew 7:7–11.

Godly Purpose

First, He developed a plan for each life,
Which He designed with delight.
For all that you are was molded from dirt,
A work of art to do His work.

Now you must give your life to Him,
So the Holy Spirit can breathe within.
Love, power, and wisdom begin to stir.
Grace is present to lift your soul to concur.

The Lord, too, will touch your lips
As He did with Jeremiah, a wonderful gift.
As the world grows in greed, destruction, and sin,
We will find comfort being with Him.

GOD'S BIBLICAL EXAMPLES

Paul built a career in this secular life,
Crucifying Christians expanding their plight.
Regan also built a fortune and fame on the earth,
Adept at inserting himself into a whir.

Apollos, a Bible-educated Jew,
Also joined the ranks of those to be used.
For helping Apollos make the accurate changes,
Pastor and teacher, Priscilla and Aquilo, are named.

Each, like many others, were chosen by God
With deliberate pre-time intention
As His magnetic infusion changed their direction.

As in our midst, is our pastor in production control,
Who yielded to the Lord instead of riches or gold.

God's Children

Born in sin,
You'd think we could not win.
But then, in time we choose
To be born again.

Whoosh, goes our sin.
We become kings for His glory,
A happy ending to this Bible story.

And all because Jesus sacrificed
So we could join Him and His Father in paradise.
If He can forgive us, so can we.
After all, we are the branches of His tree.

Inspiration from
Galatians 2:6–10.

God's Choice

First, God made Adam.
Then He made Eve
To love and conceive.

And so it is today
As the world makes its way,
A man and his bride,
Comforting each other on this roller-coaster ride.

Friends may come, and friends may go.
But there is always someone who never leaves,
Forever embedded in your mind, life, or dreams.

Two not just standing alone
For within them is the Holy Spirit's home.

Inspiration from
Ecclesiastes 4:9–10.

GOD'S CHOSEN

God's anointed are different by design.
Obstacles will not hinder what God has in mind.
No matter how they are or what they do,
The calls on their lives are made for me and you.

Don't run away or try to degrade.
Don't ridicule or judge, but render them aid.

Seek to surround yourself with their anointing
For in the midst of them is a special calling.
Like Moses or David and many others, the road is rocky,
But the reward is better than gold.

GOD'S CHURCH

That we should have a church, His home,
A haven for His people, so they won't roam.
Hear God's Word from the pastor's mouth,
Listening to every word he puts out.

And yet there is so much more.
Bring your body, soul, and spirit to the door.
Pledge your talent, time, and money.
Anything over 10 percent will make your day oh, so sunny.

Support for the efforts made to keep afloat,
Don't just paddle our own boat.
Probe your conscience and see
If you are all that you can be.

God gave you a church;
Don't make Him want to take it away.
With your love, it will survive many a day.

Inspired by
Romans 12:1–2.

GOD'S COMMUNICATION

Born again!
Make way for visions and dreams,
The way God speaks to His teams.

Write them clearly so you can share,
Motivating others to see and care.

Dying to self, paves the way
For the Lord to be a guide each day.

Patience will one day bring all into fruition.
You'll be glad you watched and waited
For the materializing of those dreams and visions.

GOD'S DESIRE

So you are living in this material world,
Gathering wealth and things of worth.
Then Jesus whispers in your ear,
"It's time to put your goodies aside and come here."

Turn what you have to God's glory divine.
Follow His plan for your life while there's still time.
If Paul were here, to you he would say,
"God's plan would go easier if you did it His way."

Those who are watching and ready to pounce
Will make your life miserable and not give an ounce.
But to be sure, where you are and what you do,
Jesus will also be there, helping you.

GOD'S FAITHFUL SOLDIERS

My father always said to be all you can be.
And when you become a soldier of the Lord,
Your dedication stands for all to see.

The Holy Spirit emanates from the inside out.
Learning is never ending and the effort intense,
To be passed on to brothers who call and shout,
"Here are the plans that Jesus laid out."

Bring in the lost at God's command,
Do it now while you can.
Reach out to all who seek to know.
The reward for faithfulness will ever grow.

GOD'S GRACE

The Lord loves you,
Not necessarily what you do
He is gracious to forgive
All sins generated as you live

But only when you are sincere
And ask from your heart with love and fear.
Know that the Lord will not remember forgiven sins,
But He will remember His plans for you.

And the size of the crown for what you do,
Watching and protecting as you follow through,
All of this is entirely up to you.

Inspiration from
Psalm 103:8–12.

God's Love Revealed

We are here but for a day.
Material things are but pleasures along the way.
What gift has been given by God, my friend?
What gift did He lend you to spend?
What plan does He have for you in this life?
To warrant the gifts He put in our care,
Do you say, "I love you (Abba) Father,"
Then go on your way?
Or do you bask in His Word
And talk to Him every day?
You were designed for His perfect plan.
Relax, submit, and take Jesus by the hand.
One doesn't have to look very far.
The Holy Spirit is in you wherever you are.
O what a delight it will be
To set our crown at the Father's feet
By walking in His Word and loving embrace
As we carry out His desires
For the short walk in this place.

Also published in my first book, *Through My Eyes,* AuthorHouse, 2008, page 3.

GOD'S PATIENCE

The patience of the Lord is not without end,
Yet His love stretches the extinguishment of men.
Still that love nurtures and protects the faithful,
For which we should be eternally grateful.

Because we all live together with good and evil,
Some may perish in this world of upheaval.

Yet one need not worry about their fate
For Jesus is never early and never late.
Into His arms we will be retrieved
And to a better place forever received.

God's Reminders

Sailing along as great as can be,
Things were good that I could see.

Then tragedy hit, and all went wrong.
What did or didn't I do?
Why should this happen to me, not you?

Suddenly, I understood my plight;
I had forgotten God and dimmed the light.

He just wanted to remind me where blessings come from.
When I turned to Him, there was the Son.

Inspiration from
Acts 27:18–26.

God's Way

First God creates children with special talents,
One day to be leaders in all circumstances.
Allowing that talent first to develop over time,
A shepherd in the making in heart and mind.

But a word of caution—if you'll listen to me—
Let the Holy Spirit lead, and you will see.
Life will be easier, and pleased the Lord will be.

For your sake, don't be like Paul,
Doing it your way in yielding to God's call.

GOD'S WILL

The Word of the Lord has no time restrictions.
The Sabbath is still honored in all conditions.
Honoring the Lord is not just in church.
Your heart will be clear in seeking and search.

One doesn't wait when there is a need,
Healing or hunger or planting a seed.

Have faith in your fellow man!
Don't judge him, but give him your hand.
What he does God may have ordained.
In due time God's will, clearly retained.

Inspiration from
Luke 6:11–16.

GOD'S WORD

Be careful what you say;
The mind and tongue can go astray.
The closer you are to the Holy Spirit,
The less chance you will err with it.

The passages meant for you
Will be clear to view,
While other parts are not meant for you.

Education may be great,
But without the Holy Spirit, errors prevail at an alarming rate.

So let God's grace abound.
His words from your mouth will sound
Like thunder from the sky,
The earth to surround.

Inspiration from
Matthew 22:23–30.

GODSENT

God designed our birth
To fulfill His plan here on earth.
Equipped with everything we need
To carry out His will and to succeed.

Even if you have no ears or eyes,
And your assets may be in disguise,
He has given us all we need
That you must recall to succeed.

The power and love of the Holy Spirit
To pick us up each time we fall,
A gift given to Christians one and all.

Inspiration from
Romans 12:1–2.

GOOD MOTHERS AND WIVES

Bathed in beauty from the inside out,
The glue that holds the family together, no doubt.
Steadfast in all circumstance,
Not willing to leave her family to chance.

Her wit and her strength in the storms of life
Are proof of her devotion as mother and wife.
Tireless, she will always adjust
By virtue of God resolutely, a must.

Like a soldier guarding over family and dome,
Beware all who would tamper with her home.
For the Lord leads her way,
Warning all enemies, "Call it a day."

GOOD OR EVIL

As you leave your old life of temporal things
That pleasure and security often bring
To focus on God and all His ways,
Which may prove difficult in the coming days …

Don't be like Lot's wife, whose heart yearned
For the pleasures that used to be.
Or you, too, may become a pillar of salt, so to speak.

Run, run as fast as you can
Into His arms, and He'll set you free,
Giving you power over evil, and victory.

GOOD WORKS

Lord, what is Your desire for me today?
What good thing should I put in play?

Here I am, Lord, give me a sign.
You have my attention in body and mind.
I'm ready to go, so don't leave me behind.

I'm ready in body and mind to do a share.
Just let me know how, when, and where.

Show me what You want that I might begin.
With hope and hard work, let the labor draw men in
To spread what is good and brighten from dim.

Inspiration from
Proverbs 13:4;
Galatians 6:9.

GRACE

Here on earth one can buy anything.
Even many people will tend to cling.

But the only way to obtain grace
Is to give your heart and life
To God in good and in strife.

To love one another as yourself,
Reevaluating your loyalty and wealth.

Living one's life according to God's plan
And influencing others by doing the best you can.

Inspiration from
Acts 8:18–25.

GRACE FOR LOYALTY

Now is the time.
This is the place.
Hear His voice.
Seek His grace!

I tell you true,
There's nothing you can do
That will replace His grace
In this worldly place.

He'll wash your sins white as snow,
And direct your life in the way to go.
And give you wisdom
You otherwise might never know.

GREAT GIFTS

Each of us has been given a special gift.
In all its beauty, the heart to lift.
Just like in marriage to become one,
Each contributing their gifts to get things done.

One may preach and another sow.
One may work in the church and another go
Into the mission field they pave,
The way for others to be saved.

Whatever talent you possess,
Do not be idle or stop to rest.
For life is short and slips by fast,
Leaving this world all too fast.

Inspiration from
Romans 12:3–8.

Growing for God

God has given gifts to all.
Among man, certain gifts will fall.
From these gifts develops God's plan
In which to serve throughout the land.

Following Jesus may bring fortune or fame.
Or you may be destined to suffer in pain.
But no matter what your fate,
You can't minister too early or too late.

Shirking your duty will endanger your reward,
And this none of us can ever afford.
So put away your doubt and fear,
And make this the best-ever year.

Inspiration from
Acts 1:2–26.
(January 3, 2016)

Hallelujah and Amen

We are imperfect from beginning to end,
But our parents love us anyway.
Hallelujah and Amen!

God knows how imperfect we really are,
But He loves us anyway, just as we are.
Hallelujah and Amen!

In order to follow our parents' and God's leads,
We need to love one another in spite of sinful deeds.
A third hallelujah and another Amen!

None is perfect except the Lord Jesus Christ.
So let's show how to love and be a guiding light.
More hallelujahs, and many Amens!

HE HAS RISEN

Our body is made in the image of Father God
While on this land we trod.
And just like Jesus on the earth,
Rose again to give us new birth.

Yet He paid a price we will never know,
Unless we choose hell as the way to go.
And as the world grows more corrupt,
He prepares a day to lift us up.

So celebrate His rise.
For then we, too, will rise again
As He opens His arms
and welcomes us in.

Inspiration from
1 Corinthians 15:1–4.

HEAVEN AT YOUR FINGERTIPS

A vision from God may not be that rare.
Even the greatest of us sinners might be made aware.
For each is born with God's plan in mind,
But whether we follow it is in the annals of time.

None is perfect save Jesus Christ.
What we do with what God has given, to be precise,
Will determine where we go after this life.

God gave us this earth, and we gave it away.
He's given us opportunity, so live life His way.
Do it, and imperfections will be overlooked each day.
Don't give the rights to heaven away.

HEAVEN'S BLESSINGS

Chorus:

I will yield, obey, and give my life to Jesus.
I will expect, react, and watch the blessings grow.
I will respond—yes respond—to the Holy Spirit
And praise the Lord for all that I have.

Verse 1:

I will yield like Saul on the road to Damascus
For I am as ready as he.
In faith, just obey as my Lord clears the way,
And I flow with the spirit every day.

Verse 2:

I will expect to receive even in adversity
For my strength comes from the Lord.
I will react when He calls to all that He asks
For the joy of the Lord is my strength.

Verse 3:

I will respond to His work and follow His plan,
The plan He made just for me.
The Holy Spirit will guide me as He grows inside me
All in the strength of His Word.

Also published in my first book, *Through My Eyes,* AuthorHouse, 2008, page 6.

HEAVEN'S CHOSEN

Perfection is heaven
Illuminated by His light.
Ever present, He eliminates the night.

And all of the spirits in there,
Spotless and clean, much aware
That only in the Lamb's Book of Life
Are their names placed with care.

Those who pledged to the Lord
And His Word did share.

Inspiration from
Revelation 21:15–27.

Help and Healing

Here we go into this world each day,
Praying, teaching, healing the Holy Spirit way.
Your job is to speak and touch,
Used by the Holy Spirit to do so much.

So your friend needed healing, and you began to pray.
Still, the healing was not on display.

Don't get discouraged for it's not up to you.
The Holy Spirit knows what He wants to do.
Just be the body He works through.

Your faith and loyalty will soon be told
As you follow God's plan, watching it unfold.
No need to fear
For the Holy Spirit is here.

Inspiration from
Acts 4:23–31.

HELPFUL HINTS

Here's what my mother said to me.
Just listen and see if you will agree.
"If you're busy with your own business,
Then there won't be time for mine."

This way temptation to judge, criticize, or condemn
Will be the furthest thing from our mind.
Perfect in this world we will never be,
Yet Jesus loves us, as you can see.

And this is what my mother said to me:
"I love you, sweet child, but not necessarily what you do.
Even for friends and foe, it remains true.
Just remember, what you do to others, someone will do to you."

Inspiration from
Matthew 7:1–6.

HE'S THE GREAT I AM

The lion and the lamb,
The beginning and the end,
Meek and pure
Is His style.

Yet strong with power,
His voice does tower.
And over us He watches
All the while.

Ruler of the universe,
King of Kings, Lord of Lords,
Son of God,
The Maker of everything.

Our Savior and our King,
The Great I Am.

HOLY FIRE

Descending upon the apostles like holy fire,
The Spirit from God brought visions and power.
Gifts did abound as they paved the way,
Continuing the work of Jesus each day.

Also, men and women, the Bible will show,
Being born again causes them to grow.
Receiving gifts of vision, prophesies, power, and might,
Evidenced in every country and tongue to right.

What an honor to be filled with grace,
To be filled with the Holy Spirit in this place.

Inspiration from
Acts 2:1–13.

HOLY SPIRIT

Apostles and believers in Christ,
Filled with the Holy Spirit to direct their life,
We're changed from within,
Trained for teaching and free of sin.

Did draw in Christians from over the land,
This is how our churches began.

A place where worship, praise, and prayer are at hand.
Where one can be nurtured and take a stand.
Where love and faith will hold,
So living for Christ shows strong and bold.

Inspiration from
Acts 2:37–47.

HOLY SPIRIT TALKS

Who but the Holy Spirit could enter in
To hearts full of selfishness and sin,
Then soften them to goodness and teaching begins.

Grace to he who yields the call
And lets the Holy Spirit control all.
What could be a more glorious way
To spend your life, leading your day?

Jesus died and rose again
To send this comforter and friend.
To lead this work to a happy end.
To those who receive Him, I say Amen.

HUMBLE PIE

Pain and suffering is the course.
Know it is the devil's force.
You can take it in stride
Knowing the Lord is by your side.

I suggest humble pie,
And here is the reason why.
The Lord was born humble;
Jesus lived and died humble.

Like Him, so should we be, you and I.
The sweet reward for humble pie
Is eternity with our Father in the sky.

Inspiration from
1 Peter 5:8–9;
James 4:13–15.

Hurricane Ike

In the big city of Houston, where I live,
Hurricane Ike came blowing in.
Great devastation began.
Trees fell, shingles flew, windows broke,
Debris grew, electricity was gone.

Darkness prolonged, and then the water came,
Flooding areas, adding to the pain; but
When it was gone, some blessings came.

Neighbor helped neighbors, and I did the same.
Cleaning and mending were all our aim.
Neighbors talked while they worked; I'm so glad.

No going to work, no computers, no TV, no hot water,
Gas lines for cars galore, no air, and
Just cooking on the grill, flashlights, and candles.
Needless to say, a whole lot more.

What do you do when there's no TV?
Why visit the neighbors, that's for me.

Also published in my first book, *Through My Eyes*, AuthorHouse, 2008, page 25.

I Am Yours

Here I am, Lord, a product of Your plan,
Unique and different in all this land.

These eyes belong to You.
These ears are Yours.

This mouth used by You.
These limbs—all for You to direct too.

Take them, Lord, for they belong to You.
Lead me, teach me, do what You will do.

Lord, here I am in plain view,
And I belong to You.

Inspiration from
Proverbs 31:30.

I JUST CAN'T SAY NO

Do I look secure to you?
Nothing could be further from the truth.
Yet the tasks you ask me to do
Would have been easier in my youth.
Even so, I just can't say no.

I practice, "No, no, no!"
But somehow, I just go, go, go.
It doesn't seem to matter how difficult the chore,
When you want it done, you come knocking at my door.
Somehow I just can't say no.

When I see you coming,
I could lock myself inside.
But there seems no place for me to hide.
The doorbell rings, the horn honks, the telephone rings.
It's still the same old song I always sing,
I just can't say no.

After I'm gone, who will take my place?
As I escape in time and space,
Will the one you choose to take my place
Do all you ask with style and grace?

Also published in my first book, *Through My Eyes,* AuthorHouse, 2008, page 22.

IF I HAD MY DRUTHERS

If I had my druthers,
I'd never see a storm.
And no one in this world
Could do another harm.

If I had my druthers,
Peace would reign everywhere.
And no one would want to harm another,
Not a single hair.

If I had my druthers,
There would never be an earthquake.
The only way the earth would move
Is with a shovel and a rake.

If I had my druthers,
No one would ever get sick.
No one would hit an animal
With any kind of stick.

If I had my druthers,
There would be food enough to go around.
It would pop everywhere from the ground.
Parents would never separate
Until they reached the heavenly gate.
If I had my druthers.

Also published in my first book, *Through My Eyes,* AuthorHouse, 2008, page 27.

The Best Poems & Poets of 2007, International Library of Poetry, 2008, page 3.

IMAGE

Here, my friend, is a thought to ponder:
Is your attitude a platitude?
Or does it come from the heart to honor
Who is your mentor, mom and dad, or other?

When we meet, will I turn and run?
Or will I stretch my arms and encourage you to come?
Will I seek your beauty and advice?
Will I think that you are honest and nice?

No matter what goes on in life,
Be it good or bad, great or strife,

God has placed the Holy Spirit inside
To reach your heart and test your pride.
For everything you do,
Remember, God is watching you.

Inspiration from
Isaiah 1:18;
Proverbs 27:17.

IN CHRIST

How awesome can it be
That Christ took our sins and set us free?

But we are not adopted yet.
And here is a reminder, lest we forget.

First we must ask God to forgive our sin,
Open our hearts, and let the Holy Ghost in.
To become His child, denounce future sin.

Begin anew from the inside out.
Tell all the world what He's about.
Lift our voices to praise and shout.

For we are in Him and He in us.
On earth and in heaven, eternal righteousness.

In God's Hands

Rejecting the Holy Spirit is rejecting the Lord.
You think you can prosper all by yourself;
You think you don't need the Lord's help.

A warning to all: It will be done unto you as you do unto others.
Even mothers, fathers, sisters, and brothers.
Oh yes, you reap what you sow—
Good, bad, happy, or sad.

Glory is not yours, so don't sing your own song.
For Jesus will right all you do wrong.
He will focus on all His children as we focus on Him
For He is the great I Am.

IN BUT NOT OF THIS WORLD

I once was lost, but now I'm found.
In a land divided, I'll stand my ground.
Successfully living with the rules of this land,
Yet faithfully exposing God's loving hand.

Simply follow the rules of the road,
While setting the example that God did unfold.
Show the world cheerfully every day
How great it is when God's work is in play.

INSPIRED WORD

Inspiration for the godly comes from the Bible,
And those who believe it will not be idle.
No one like the Pharisees can detour
Those who have opened to the Spirit forever more.

Reading the Bible brings wisdom and joy
As the Lord's Word springs forth all answers
To any problem and all.
The Bible is written for the simple in mind,
So none would be left behind.

But woe to he who would interpret or ignore
The purpose of any passage of inspiration from the Lord.
Let the Holy Spirit be your guide,
And all fear will then subside.

Inspiration from
2 Timothy 3:10–17.

INTIMIDATION

You know something I don't know?
Tell me, tell me so I, too, can grow.
Or are you afraid to teach me or make me wise?
Would I be a threat in your eyes?
That for me to learn would take your role?

Remember how Saul felt about David?
This story is told in our Bible so sacred.

Maybe we could share a thing or two.
I know that God would want us to.
He has placed us together for a season,
Teaching each other could be a part of the reason.

Jealousy and intimidation are a sin, but humility
Will bring forgiveness over and over again.

We all have talents we were given to share,
To spread them here and to spread them there.
If you turn me down, I'll just move to another.
And we'll never get to really know each other.

Our talents together could have greater things made.
But instead, they become not color but shadows of shade.

Also published in my first book, *Through My Eyes,* AuthorHouse, 2008,
page 38.

KNOW GOD

No man is perfect, this He understands.
But the Holy Spirit is there to help each man.
To comfort and guide those who love the Lord,
To use the Word as a powerful sword.

His love and guidance lie deep inside,
Where your heart and soul do reside.
Prayers spoken to God in Jesus's name
Are answered when the time is right.

So don't hesitate to call on His name.
For His answer may come one fine night.
Or it just may come on a peaceful morn.
But always, always when the time is right.

Inspiration from
John 14:15–21.

Also published in my first book, *Through My Eyes*, AuthorHouse, 2008,
page 17.

LEADERSHIP

To lead the lost that they might see
All that God has planned them to be.
To give to a brother in need
From the heart to help him succeed.

Brings pleasure to the Lord
And strikes for Him the perfect chord.

So do not be dismayed.
Nor be disheartened or afraid
When used, abused, or feel betrayed
For the Lord will reward your way.

LEGACY

What happened to all the ambition
That disappeared with the evolution of time?
What happened to all the desires
That youth conspires to find?

Yesterday has come and gone.
Today is but a fleeting glance.
Tomorrow is too far away,
And I seem to get lost in the games of chance.

What will I leave behind to encourage a child
That in all of this world life is worthwhile?
This is the answer, not nearly profound,
To love one another is the best common ground.

Take the God-given talents you have at hand,
And spread them generously across the land.

Also published in my first book, *Through My Eyes,* AuthorHouse, 2008,
page 19.

LIFE

Life is what you make it, they say.
Of course it depends on influence along the way.
Some of you might consider good and some bad
And how much of each you've had.

How you respond would indeed come in play
For you need to handle them in just the right way.
Your age could determine if you win or lose,
Depending on whether it was big or small in your mind.
Would it affect your future, or could you leave it behind?

Wow, I never thought about it before.
Now life could be complicated forevermore.

Also published in my first book, *Through My Eyes,* AuthorHouse, 2008,
page 21.

LIFE IS A CHALLENGE

With Mom and Dad, how safe you feel.
No matter what you do, they love you still.
Yet when you do wrong, correction is at hand.
To avoid this conflict, you do the best you can.

To keep you on a good solid course
Are teachers, preachers, and authorities in force.
You may choose your way
But generally guided from day to day.

Picture this—a Father in heaven and a father on earth.
The Holy Spirit to guide your spiritual worth.
Mentors and authorities for your time here,
While never forgetting the Holy Spirit is near.

Put on your armor and sharpen your ear
For the Holy Spirit and protection from fear.

Inspiration from
Philippians 3:14;
James 1:8.

LIFE NEEDS

Life is but a fleeting glance,
And each moment needs to be enhanced.
Rise in the morning with a smile,
Praise the Lord, and visit with Him awhile.

Plan your day with enthusiastic style.
Show the world one of the creations He made,
And watch that enthusiasm does not fade.

For those who are drawn to your side,
Let the Lord be known both far and wide.
They will see how beautiful and precious life is
With a smile, song, pat, or even a kiss.

Inspiration from
Lamentations 3:22;
2 Corinthians 5:17.

LIFE ON EARTH

Life on earth is but a fleeting glance.
Forge ahead, and take a chance.
Family, strangers, and friends may come and go
As the Lord sees fit to help you grow.

In order to ride out the tide,
One must let the Holy Spirit guide.
Stick close, stick tight with all your might,
Then you will sleep in peace every night.

Inspiration from
Deuteronomy 31:6;
Philippians 3:8.

LIFE WITHIN

Division brings out the racists.
Combined, we are riddled with chaos.

Equality stifles progress
As the devil beguiles even the wise.
A wolf in sheep's clothing for disguise
Will result in our demise.

So where can we turn?
Look within and learn,
For it's the Holy Spirit's turn.

He'll show you what no man can teach
And take you to heights man alone cannot reach.

Inspiration from
Galatians 5:22–23.

LIFE'S CHALLENGE

Do not fear adversity.
The Lord is beside you for all to see.

Follow what He is doing as He leads the way.
As He seeks the oppressed, and you teach them to pray.

See the miracles to behold,
And watch His glory before you unfold.

For He has given you all you need
To spread His Word and plant His seed.

LITTLE CHILDREN

Little children are the apples of His eye.
Innocent yet guilty makes me wonder why.

There is, however, one thing that I know.
They need to be directed toward the Lord
As they begin to grow.

For they must learn to love and depend on Him.
So as they grow, God's plan for them
Will be revealed and can begin.

LORD JESUS, I LOVE YOU

Lord Jesus, I love You, but I can't count the ways.
You're the maker of my dreams, the love within my soul.
You're in me and on me, all-around me, oh Lord.
And I love You, but I can't count the ways.

You're in the air I breathe, the life I live.
You're in the songs I sing, the light for all to see.
I want the world to know that You're a part of me.
But if You were to ask me, Lord,
I'd say I love You, but I can't count the ways.

Also published in my first book, *Through My Eyes,* AuthorHouse, 2008, page 8.

LOVE AND LOYALTY

Love and loyalty is a condition.
But the Holy Spirit will help the vision.
You say you're born again!
Then look who now lives within.

So let the Holy Spirit reign,
And nothing will ever be the same.
He'll open your heart and mind,
Leaving a cold heart and confusion behind.

He'll allow His gifts to come rushing through.
The more faithful you grow, the more you do.
Don't just believe but say.
Don't just wish but act and pray.

Inspiration from
Acts 4:10–20.

LOVE IS GOD

The spirit of God lays within you,
Creating a bond of love.
Through dreams, pictures, language, and song,
The Spirit does transfer to you all day long.

The love of God to all humankind,
In fruit and flowers and mates divine.
Don't ever let the Spirit go
For within lays the power God did bestow.

LOVE IS LIFE

If you love Me, feed My sheep.
The meaning of this is very deep.
Love your neighbor as yourself,
Giving any talent and help.

Make the love of God inside of me.
Surface and set it free.
Let me lead the way
By serving and teaching every day.

Even better yet, lest I forget,
Is to be open to the teachings
From the Bible and chosen preaching.
Amen.

Inspiration from
1 Peter 4:7–11.

LOVE, LOVE

Love is the basis of all things.
One cannot see it, hear it, taste it, feel it, or smell it.
But through the grace of God, in love the heart sings.

Love has great power to overcome.
Confident it will grow because of where it comes from,
Conquering the sorrows and sin on this earth and under the sun.

All else is powerless and in vain.
Without love, all else is fruitless gain.

Also published in my first book, *Through My Eyes,* AuthorHouse, 2008, page 47.

LOVING HIM

Love is the unselfish desire to please another.
It makes the heart sing to see joy in a brother,
Wipe away a baby's tears,
And to build a crown throughout the years.

To present to your Father, the King of Kings,
Not earthly treasures of diamond and rings
But deeds that show worship and praise,
The music for His ears throughout your days.

And using the talent He placed in you
Is the greatest gift that you could do.

LOYALTY

Jesus died for you and me,
And we would die for our family.
We would die to protect our land.
But for Jesus, would we take a stand?

In church we sing and pray.
But in a week, that's only one day.
Jesus sent a comforter in the Holy Ghost
To be your guide and host.

Know that He is with you every day
And stands beside you, come what may.
Do not fear a martyr to be,
For this kind of bravery is for you and me.

Inspiration from
Acts 7:51–60.

MANY GIFTS

The Lord gives each many gifts to display.
The greatest is the Holy Spirit to show the way.
Use your God-given talent to plant the seeds,
Knowing with the Lord you shall succeed.

Recognize what the Holy Spirit has begun.
Join Him till the purpose is done.
For if you concentrate on the purpose of Him,
Life will be better and evil be dim.

Think of you and the Holy Spirit as a team,
And He'll use your talent to accomplish the dream.

Inspiration from
Mark 8:36;
1 Corinthians 12:4–6.

MARY OR MARTHA

Mary and Martha loved Jesus, showing it each in a different way.
Neither was wrong when He came that day.
What's in the heart will clearly unfold,
And how you show it is bound to take hold.

Whether you live in a tent with a dirt floor
Or in a place with treasures galore.

And on my mother's door you could plainly see
A sign that said, "If you want to see my house, make an appointment,
But if it's me you wish to see, come anytime if you please!"

MUSIC TO HIS EARS

Music and an ode to our Father,
Coming from the depths of our heart.
From the beginning of time to forever,
Music has been there from the start.

It can be heard from the rustle of leaves,
The songs of birds in the trees,
The ocean waves on a silent night,
The sound of a choir is sheer delight.

Or the sound of insects chirping in the dark
Lends to the submission of worship in the heart.
Oh, those instruments God did create,
And the talent to play them ever so great.

All instruments and voices in harmony, I have found,
Expands our worship to heights that are heaven bound.

MY LORD

Here is to Your body,
And here is to Your blood.
Monthly I celebrate
Your sacrifice in love.

I celebrate Your birthday,
I celebrate Your end,
Grateful that You love men.

I'll say it over and over again,
"Hooray, hallelujah, and Amen."

MY MEADOW

Over in a meadow, tall and green,
Lying in the middle, not to be seen.
The clouds slowly passing by,
Each clearly separate from a blue, blue sky.

No honking horns, no noisy din.
No one watching; no one can.
No hurry, no rush, only to be aware
Of the breeze gently blowing through the air.

Rustling leaves caressing me so.
Please don't tell anyone you know.
Drifting peacefully off to sleep,
Thinking this is a place I'd love to keep.

Also published in my first book, *Through My Eyes*, AuthorHouse, 2008, page 17.

MY PRAYER

Lord, bathe me in Your wisdom and strength.
Help me to be all that You want me to be.
Let my enemies respect the You that is in me.

Help me to find peace in a world filled with evil,
How to deal with the works of the devil.

Hold me, Lord, as I make my way
Through the dense maze we face each day.
Let me be a light to those in need
And not be sidetracked by power or greed.

Let not my enemy overpower me
But reciprocate the peace they see.
Let all Christians unite in faith to agree.

Inspiration from
Proverbs 16:18;
Romans 12:14.

MY PRAYER OF LOVE

Lord, there isn't a day goes by
When I don't feel Your touch.

Lord, there isn't a day goes by
When I don't sense Your love.

Lord, there isn't a day goes by
That I don't see Your works.

Lord, there isn't a day goes by
That You don't heal my hurts.

Lord, there isn't a day goes by
That You don't keep my life on track.

Lord, there isn't a day goes by
That I don't love You back.

Your child and faithful servant.

NEVER ALONE

Eve was fashioned for Adam,
A woman to be a companion to man.
An example of how we were not to be alone,
A single person destitute and unknown.

But to cohabit across this land,
Nurturing and assisting as best we can.

Loving and caring for all in our path,
Protecting from harm, misfortune, and wrath.
So may the grace of the Lord fill your day,
And pass all God's love to whoever passes your way.

Inspiration from
Acts 23:31.

No Arguing; Just Do It

Never condemn, complain, or criticize is my motto.
When God fits you into His plan, just be ready to follow.

How much adversity will you take in
Before you happily follow Him?

Not like a sheep that has lost his way,
But like one who has found God's given forte.

No Other

Praise to Jesus, the lion and the Lamb,
Overseer of all that was and is to be,
The great I Am.

He died for you and me,
And then rose from death victoriously.
And we stand by Him in defeat of the enemy.

My life, my King of Kings,
My soul to Him I gladly bring.
For only Jesus in proven power and goodness,
Could open the sealed scroll of God,
Revealing His plan for the times in its fullness.

Now with Humble Pie

Riches and power can enlarge the head;
A fall from grace can put it to bed.
Using God's gifts can result in fame,
But all must know from whence it came.

Then when God's children cry out in sorrow,
He'll heal them today or tomorrow.
Each day has its own needs to fill.
Solving today's needs today is God's advice and His will.

Your growth in the Lord will clearly show
By the way He has used you for all to know.

OBEDIENCE

God sent His Son to save the world.
Preplanned, His life was to unfurl.
Obediently, Jesus went His way each day,
Following His Father's direction in every way.

As a result, the Holy Spirit helps us out
To do the preplanned will of God each day,
Each prepared in a separate and unique way,
The reason we seek the Holy Spirit and pray.

Just remember that He was pure and clean,
And we are both good, bad, and in between.

He died on a cross and rose again.
We, however, live for today, never knowing the end,
Of which we know not where or when.

Inspiration from
Matthew 2:19–23.

ONLY THE FACTS

Like the captain of his ship
Or a pilot flying his plane,
History is recorded as proved
Through witness maintained.

Luke, as a doctor, gathered all the facts,
And putting them in logical order,
Recorded all the proper acts.
So history went forward.

First, John the Baptist was born,
With the Holy Ghost inside,
To plant the seeds for Jesus to arrive.

Our Obedience

The church is the rock that Jesus builds.
We are the caretakers and doers of His will.
As we follow His will and His ways,
He will bless and protect the church in coming days.

Jesus doesn't throw money from the sky.
Let me tell you the reason why.
He has given to each of us talent and worth
And designated a part for the church.

Yes, and if we do not support the church's attempt to raise funds,
Then the beginning of the end will have begun.
If we neglect His home,
Then He will leave us to stand alone.

Inspiration from
Matthew 16:13–20.

PARADISE

The streets of heaven are made of gold;
This is what I have always been told.
But why should I care for silver and gold?
Those are earthly things and, oh, so cold.

My home will be the universe,
And my love of God will always be first.

He'll open the gate and wave me in.
Finally I'll be free of pain and sorrow,
Including enemies and sin.
A whole new life will then begin.

PATH TO HEAVEN

Being born again is clearly a must,
Easily done without fanfare or fuss,
A pledge of the heart from each of us.

Next comes baptism; baptism, what can one say?
Outwardly, a dedication to God on display,
A family affair put in play.

Last but not least, in order to grow,
We should seek to follow Jesus
Wherever He will go.
The reason for birth we hopefully know.

The more of Him one seeks,
The more He'll reveal for you to know
Through the Holy Spirit placed inside
That rapidly begins to grow.

Putting this together, my friend,
Is up to you as to where and when.
So open the door, and let the Holy Spirit in.
The path to heaven will then begin.

PERSONIFIED

Jesus is perfection personified,
Something we cannot be.
Even the angels cannot be
For they need direction, like you and me.

Jesus was born to teach and pave the way.
Died on a cross to save the day.
He even stood fast before His enemy,
Not succumbing to temptation to set us free.

Then Jesus arose to take God's hand,
Sitting omnipotent by God's side,
As only He can,
Sending the Holy Spirit to you and me.

Now Father, Son, and Holy Ghost.
Three in one, the blessed Trinity.

PLEASING GOD

An attitude of gratitude,
Of this I do attest.
For obedience to His commands
Puts my heart and mind at rest.

Knowing it will bring rewards
Excites me to the core
As the Lord opens every door,
Which Satan cannot ignore.

My tithes and offerings will soar
And set me on His path forevermore.

Inspiration from
Malachi 3:10–12.

PLEASING JESUS

When you follow Jesus,
Your very essence fills the room.
More will want to follow
Than wish you pain and doom.

Reach out and take their hand.
Lead them to the Promised Land,
Where enemy and strife have no place.
And they, too, can follow Jesus with style and grace.

Inspiration from
Matthew 5:13–16.

POSSESSIONS

All that I have, Lord, belongs to You.
All that I am belongs to You too.
Bearing that in mind, this is what I do.

Taking care of all You've given to me
And being all You want me to be.

Nothing, nothing will I hold back.
Even when I sin or get off track,
The Holy Spirit pulls me back.
And I am grateful He keeps me on track.

I will respect the things He gives to me,
Including shared things from sea to sea.
Even my profound love for Him He'll always see
Until the day I cease to be.

Inspiration from
Acts 5:1–11.

PRAISE THE LORD

First He made you with a plan.
Then He placed you in this land.

In death, He took away your sin
If only you would believe in Him.

He gave you the Holy Ghost
And the power for which to host.

Praise the King of Kings
And all faith in what He brings.

Celebrate the Lord
With prayer, song, and dance in one accord.

Inspiration from
Luke 19:32–40.

PRAY IN THE SPIRIT

Satan appears to be winning the battle,
But he won't herd us like sheep or cattle.
Put on your armor of truth and righteousness,
The gospel of peace.
Have a pure heart with salvation and faith that will not cease.

Speak the Word of God, the sword of the Spirit.
Open your mouth so all can hear it.
The armor is preparation,
But prayer is the battle against Satan.

Prayer and singing in the Spirit
Glorify the Father and Son.

You will be heard.
As ambassadors, we speak it loud and clear
For all the world to hear.

Inspiration from
Ephesians 6:10–18.

PREPARE FOR JESUS

What? Your world is not full of silver and gold?
Well maybe you can't have that to have life unfold.

Into God's plan for your life and all you must do,
A truly God-given plan just for you.

One you cannot be given without difficulties and strife.
But then, before you know it, you'll receive great things in eternal life.

PROPHECIES OF GOD

The Lord knows all things.
In the Bible, His Word, these prophecies He brings.
Peter predicted to deny Jesus three times,
And oh, so many more in the Bible we find.

Like Jude's deception was enacted.
Oh, what a web we can weave
When in the practice to deceive.

How many of you practice what we are not?
What do we lose or gain in forming a plot?

Jacob and his mother may have deceived the blind,
But God had control in the annals of time.

PUSHING FORWARD

When nothing goes right, and everything goes wrong,
Hope springs eternal when worshipping in song.
God inserted assets when you were born;
You may use them to toot your own horn.

Or use them as He did intend,
To teach heaven, love, and hope to men.
Heaven looms in the distance,
While surrounded by resistance,
For those children of God who persevere.

READY FOR JESUS

It's never too late before Jesus comes
For each of us to examine what we have done
And make the changes to the glory of the Son.

Open your heart, brave the storms,
Seek shelter in His loving arms.
Bask in His Word, and sound the alarm.

For when Jesus comes on His white horse,
We will be ready to follow His course
As bathed in His blood, He comes with force.

This spiritual warfare did
Into the lake of fire cast Satan and followers.
And the final victory is ours.

Inspiration from
Revelation 19:11–21

REMEMBER ME

A supper by Jesus of great proportion
From which a covenant was born.
So beware of any other notion.
Of this be advised and warned.

The bread and wine depict His body and blood,
Remembering the cross He endured for you and me
To take away our sins and set us free.
We take this bread and wine in remembrance of Him.

And let the church gather to be sure,
Believing and thinking of Jesus, who did endure.
As often as you partake and agree,
Take this covenant seriously for all to see
And do it only in remembrance of me.

Inspiration from
1 Corinthians 11:23:32.

RESPONSIBILITY

When I was young, my mother cleared the way.
When I was older, I was to clear my day.
My parents said there are others in this home,
And each responsible for his own.

Take this philosophy to the street
For employers, friends, strangers, and everyone you meet.
Consider all in what you do.
Don't leave a mess for them to remember you.

Set the example in all you say and do.
Then many followers will be drawn to you.

Inspiration from
Ephesians 5:4;
1 Corinthians 13:11.

ROLLER-COASTER WORLD

Sometimes you have money;
Sometimes you don't.
Sometimes you work,
And sometimes you won't.

Sometimes you're happy;
Sometimes you're sad.
Sometimes you're good;
Sometimes you're bad.

Sometimes you're healthy;
Sometimes you're sick.

If you can get out of "sometimes,"
That would be a good trick.
Yet whether up or down,
The Holy Spirit can always be found.

RULES AND PROMISES

God gave this earth to us without fanfare or fuss.
Then we immediately fell into sin.
Not exactly the way to begin.

So we could start over again,
God sent His Son to rid us of sin.
But here we go, basking in sin again.

Love like God's for which we should strive,
As long as we are on earth and alive.
Didn't God even send the Holy Spirit to help?
If you are in tune, you can easily tell.

According to His Bible promise revealed and is seen,
He will punish the sinner, rescue the follower,
And wipe the earth oh so clean.

Inspiration from
Micah 5:1–5.

SEE MY HEART, OH LORD

Lord, I feel Your pain
While some trade obedience for gain.
Or abandon Your love when
The devil comes to call.
Or don't acknowledge You at all.

But I'm here, oh Lord!
Let Your Spirit in me be of one accord.
Speak to me, oh Lord.

Show me Your way.
Teach me Your will every single day.
I am Your servant and will always be subservient.
See my heart, oh Lord, lead me in Your way.

Servants of the Lord

Jesus was a teacher and servant,
A sample for all to see.
Also there are the chosen, like you and me.

To be given this honor by God and man
Brings joy and desire to do the best you can.
What a service we are allowed to be,
Rewarding now is what you see.

But rewards to come we've yet to know.
Still we serve to grow and grow.
How good you can feel to be chosen by God and man
To serve in churches throughout the land.

Inspiration from
Acts 6:1–7.

SHOO, SHOO, DEVIL

Shoo, shoo, devil,
You can't come in!
Shoo, shoo, devil,
Here you cannot win.

This is the place that Jesus made.
This is the place where souls are saved.
This is the place where love is found,
And where the Holy Spirit walks 'round.

So shoo, shoo, devil, you can't come in!

Also published in my first book, *Through My Eyes,* AuthorHouse, 2008, page 9.

SIMPLE PRAYER

The prayer of every Christian—
No matter what religion,
In the Bible is clearly given,
An example dearly written.
"Our Father who art in heaven."

How much more complete could it be?
First a focus on Him before a focus on me.
And back to Him, you see.

He knows of all your needs,
He knows of all your wants.
While His need is for your undivided love
And to follow His direction from above.

SPIRIT-FILLED

Demons lurking all around,
Looking for a home.
Evil in your mind and heart
Are demons' stomping ground.

Beware when you're in contact
With one who's demon-filled.
Keep Jesus in your heart and head,
Or that demon may favor you instead.

So repent your sins.
Always stay faithful and close.
Then He will protect you forever,
And never let you go.

Spirit Renewal

Revive Your spirit within me, oh Lord.
Let my soul and Your Spirit be in one accord.
Let my adrenalin rise
As my face reaches toward the sky.

And my voice echoes Your desire
As my heart seeks to aspire.

I will speak of You to the wind
To the trees to babies and to men
Over and over, again and again.
And only then will I have begun.

Spirit, Soul, and Body

My body may yield to sin.
My soul may submit to sin.
But my spirit belongs to Father God,
And that will always be with Him.

The world can sin around me
And even do me wrong.
But turning to the Holy Spirit
Brings me peace through prayer and song.

I see where He is working; I seek what He wants.
I join Him always searching
In all the ways that count.

Spreading the Word

Rise and shine.
Give the Lord some time.
Now that you're ready for the day,
Let the world know what you want to say.

Put on your smile, sing, and shout
In all its glory 'round about
That this is the day the Lord has made.
Let people know they can be saved.

Full of grace in all you do, and if they reject your plea,
Dust yourself off, and you will see
Some soil is bad and some good.
Yet you spread that seed as best you could.

Inspiration from
Romans 3:23; 6:23; 5:8; 10:9.

Stormy Weather

Life is like a roller-coaster ride and
Obstacles coming from back and side.
Faith in God helps weather the storm
From lies, deception, and so much more.

Just when you think you're at the top,
Out comes the foundation, and down you drop.

But here is the good news from me to you:
Remember God's Word in all you do.
And when it comes to the end of our days,
You'll walk with the Lord in love and grace.

STRETCH FOR JOY

How do we find joy in a world of power, pain, anger, and sorrow?
When the promises of today will never be better tomorrow?
Chaos strikes in every corner.
Life today will soon become the former.

Freedom rapidly deemed obsolete,
And the right to anything will be a treat.
The world crumbles beneath our feet.
People starve with no food to eat.
Many have become indifferent to life and death,
Not so much as a flinch or fret.

As I see it, the only thing to do
Is put on a big smile just for you.
Knowing that God is by our side
As He prepares for those who do abide.
A world where evil does not exist,
And each throws the other a great big kiss.

Strong in the Lord

Don't just call on the Lord when you have a need.
Die to self, and plant His seed.
He is your Father, so pray with love to Him,
With an earnest endeavor to begin.

Talk to Him throughout the day.
Let all see Him in you along the way.
Show the Lord just who you are.
To His glory you can be His budding star.

Yield to the Holy Spirit that lies within.
Set His words on your tongue and begin.

The day will come when He will say,
"Well done, faithful servant, come this way;
My arms await your spirit this day."

Inspiration from
Jeremiah 29:11–13.

Suffer for God

Our body and mind may suffer
Slings and arrows of fellow man.
But the Spirit of God lies in us,
Strengthening our endurance again and again.

Jesus's body may have died on the cross,
Yet His Spirit lies within, never to be a loss.
He continues within you and me,
Including the suffering meant to be.

You can plainly see the extension of Jesus
Through the likes of you and me.
And maybe one day, too, hang upon a tree.

Inspiration from
2 Corinthians 4:7–12.

SUPERPOWER

When you've reached the end of the trail,
When you've gone as far as you can go,
Then will you call upon the Lord
For the superpower that will never fail.

Wouldn't it be better to seek Him from the start,
Go get His help and approval?
After all, the Holy Spirit is a layer in your heart
And yearns for you to call.

He waits patiently to hear from you,
To be a part of all you do,
To carry you to the heights of God's plan,
Enabling you with power beyond any man.

TELL ME WHY

Why is man always struggling to control everything and everyone,
Aggressively pursuing in the dead of night or with the sun?
Destroying all the beauty 'round about,
Killing any love that might come out.

Until all the world is fully gray,
And all beauty and good is passed away.
Till all men are like animals of prey.
Until nothing is left for them to take away.

Maybe they will destroy each other with nothing left to pursue.
Then we can rebuild the world anew,
Just God and me and you.

Also published in *International Who's Who in Poetry (XII) 2012*,
page 146.

Temptation

The Holy Spirit will help you discern
What brains and emotions cannot learn.
Tears are not always sorrow,
And laughter can delude for tomorrow.

Sin has many forms, the Bible warns.
Sin is but for a moment and then after to mourn.
Every deed has its price.
While evil casts shadows, good is warm and nice.

Gratification tends to be short and sweet.
Then disaster replaces that treat.

But good lingers like ripples in a pond,
Bringing warmth and joy to those who look on
As the essence of the Lord is revealed in the pond.

TEST MY HEART

Test my heart to see if it's true
That I will laugh and cry with you.

Test and see if I won't share God's view
Of an uplifted spirit and prayer
To bring you through.

And the more God gives me,
The more I have to share.
He is so generous with you and I
That there's often more to spare.

Yet since we share our lives
As sister and brother,
We both have the same wonderful cover.

Inspiration from
Proverbs 4:24.

TESTING

Here was a boyfriend my parents should like.
As soon as they met, I knew I was right.
Perhaps we could test the waters by living together a while,
Make sure there would be no divorce after a walk down the aisle.

My parents were opposed, you could plainly see.
Reluctantly unhappy, they promised to be
Silent long enough to watchfully see.

But then came his birthday,
And much to our surprise
Came his birthday cake,
With a bride and groom to try on for size.

Also published in my first book, *Through My Eyes,* AuthorHouse, 2008, page 45.

THANKSGIVING

We thank God for all He has given us
Every day of the year.
But what about those around us
And the ones we hold dear?

Friends and family, acquaintances alike,
It takes all of us together to do it right.
Planting, taking care of, and harvesting each day,
From beginning to end, we do our part this way.

Now we come together to harvest
What we have sown,
And thank the Lord for these gifts
Which we use to make our happy home.

The Adventurous Spirit

The adventurous ones grow in fame and fortune,
To me there is no doubt.
If you don't want to be left behind,
It's time you figured that out.

Look at Christopher Columbus; don't you agree?
He was an example for all to see.
For his adventurous spirit, yes siree,
You'll find him in the books of history.

How about the presidents throughout time?
Each made decisions over the land.
They were important, you will find.
We witnessed their works firsthand.

Think of what you could do, my friend.
How about a poem now and then?
Or maybe a painting that withstands time,
A painting to express, like a poem that rhymes.

Also published in my first book, *Through My Eyes*, AuthorHouse, 2008, page 16.

THE CHALLENGE

You can put me in prison
Or shake my tree.
Still my voice will rise in song and plea,
The words of my Lord to echo in me.

You can take my head,
Put my life to bed.
But my Lord's Word will rise
Through the air over the skies.

And fall firmly across the land
To rescue the lost at God's command.
I want all to see
That fear is not a part of me.

Inspiration from
Acts 26:24–32.

THE COVENANT

Salvation to all of us
Without sacrifice or cost.
Sins all forgiven
That none should be lost.

Jesus to sacrifice only once,
Freeing us from sin and lust.
Believe and follow for time is short,
Then the chance is gone forever more.

THE CUP OF LIFE

The world is full of beauty.
One can see it everywhere.
And parts are so breathtaking,
I can only sit and stare.

Yet the most beautiful of all
Is being fashioned after Him.
So let's not waste another moment
From the inside out.

While we follow in His footsteps,
Let's sing, dance, and shout.
Pray in reverent honor to Him and for one another
For God made us all as a sister and a brother.

Inspiration from
Psalm 50:9–2.

THE CYCLE OF LIFE

Born in sin, we do proceed,
Quickly learning what we need.

Crying gets us everywhere,
Satisfaction all in all,
A trait we widely share.

As we grow, how clever we are,
Manipulation our budding star.

We quickly learn Mom and Dad want to please.
We know how to use this with surprising ease.
All too soon it's time to leave home,
Suddenly finding ourselves on our own.

Our dream is to reach the sky,
feeling our way as we try.
It's only then we learn the truth
Of all the mistakes we made in our youth.

Raised like a child of royalty,
Losing the crown, giving up our ways,
We roll up our sleeves and labor each day.

Through hard work and little play,
Vowing to teach our children a much different way.

Also published in *Best Poets of 2014*, vol. 3, Ebert & Wein Publishing, page 222.

THE DECLINING DREAM

America, the home of the free!
A place where one can be
Whatever they want to be.
Or at least that's what we used to see.

Wars and the power-hungry
Who think they are wiser than anyone else,
Through lies and deception,
Put our desires on the shelf.

And we have become slaves
Without the use of a belt.
The Bible tells me this is the way it will be.
But still I cry in the land of the free.

The Faithful Christian

A Christian may be kidnapped
Or even lose their head.
Not to run or cower but to
Stand bravely instead.

Going where most dare to go,
Living the life every Christian would know.
Letting God lead the way,
Being grateful for each passing day.

Praying for each other.
Building up each sister and brother.

Inspiration from
Acts 12:1–5.

THE FINAL ACT

First, He came of flesh, like you and me,
Raised in this world till thirty-three.

Then His work began,
Preaching and teaching throughout this land.

Healing and miracles could be seen
Wherever He appeared on the scene.

Then His persecution and death began
To take away the sins of man.

To complete the task, He rose from the dead
To send a Comforter—the Holy Spirit—in His stead.

Inspiration from
Luke 24:1–35.

THE GREATEST CHALLENGE

Love your neighbor as yourself,
Not what he does nor his wealth.
Conduct yourself like Jesus would,
Living in love and doing good.

Jesus suffered with His life,
Enduring pain and strife.
Never faltering, never changing,
Always strong but humble in His life.

He paid the price so you could stand with Him,
A light in the world so dark and grim.
If you do not falter in the goal,
In the end, all happiness and glory will unfold.

Inspiration from
1 Peter 2:9–12.

THE GREATEST GIFT

To seek Jesus, to know Him, to love Him.
The greatest gift, I do believe,
A child could ever hope to receive
Is to find Him in the arms of family and friends.

To know and celebrate His birth
And the reason He came to this earth.

Remember, Santa comes just once a year.
But Jesus, our greatest gift, is always here.

The Lord, Holy Spirit, and You

From the first breath to the last,
Our future is cast.
Whether we follow His plan or not
Will be seen in what we do, not what we've got.

So use your talents, and share with others.
Extend Jesus's love to sisters and brothers.
What you do and give come shining through;
The Lord will reward for all you do.

As long as you remember it comes from Him
And not from you.
Pray and praise the Lord, and
Listen to the Holy Spirit for they are in one accord.

Inspiration from
Acts 9:36–43.

THE LORD'S CHOSEN

God's chosen are in this world but not of this world,
Here to let God's Word and ways be heard.
The church is the place to teach and learn,
Where all do gather for work and concern.

A place of worship and prayer,
A place to grow in love and care,
A place to renew and face each trial.

As we work to live in Jesus's footsteps and style
And boldly proclaim the way all the while.

Inspiration from
Luke 10:25–37.

THE LORD'S WORD

The words of our Lord are true and clear,
Never changing from year to year.
Yet not everyone can understand,
Giving way to interpretation across the land.

Seek out those who God has assigned
To accurately explain each line.
For those who listen, the Holy Spirit speaks.
Will bar confusion and inaccurate leaks.

Inspiration from
Acts 18:24–28.

THE LOVE SACRIFICE

Jesus prayed to His Father not for fear of death
but for the reasons why.
On His knees He prayed with His face to the sky.
Those who went with Jesus to the garden slept.

Like babes, oblivious to pain and suffering to be,
The reason and the way that set us free.

Is this an example of how we could be,
Unfeeling for the suffering of others
Or the sacrifice Jesus made for you and me?

Or is Jesus the perfect example of obedience,
Love, and bond with us, Father and Son,
All that we should be when life has begun?

Inspiration from
Matthew 26:36–41.

THE RIGHT GENEROSITY

Generosity comes from the heart.
Those born again have a good start.
Yet how close do we get to the Holy Spirit?
Knowing He is there won't make you hear it.

Jesus has given you the gift of love.
This gift comes only from heaven above.
Let the Holy Spirit lead the way.
Rise each morning determined to bless the day
In some warm, caring, and generous way.

Too often we offer the fish instead of the fishing pole,
Multiplying the need and confusing the goal.
A fact to remember:
God must bless before we can surrender.

Inspiration from
Corinthians 8:1–8.

THE ROCK

Do you feel powerless or weak?
Do your dreams seem hard to seek?

Praise the Lord down on your knees.
Speak to the Lord as you feel His breeze.

A breeze that caresses your upward face
With a pleasing smile, His blessing and grace.

There lies your power and gain,
A power that only faith can attain.

Seek it on a rock, the church of His choice.
Then seek Him in that small inner voice.

THE TEST OF LOVE AND FAITH

The sin of Hosea's day is much like today,
Corruption everywhere plaguing our way.
Guard your heart lest evil and hardness creep in,
Allowing acceptance of lust and sin.

Like God, Hosea's love did prevail.
Over mountains of turmoil, it did steadily sail.
Like a parent with a wayward child,
Love never ends in spite of the trials.

Stay close to God so the Holy Spirit can help,
Holding constant faith, never to be placed on a shelf.
This is God's challenge to you and me.
So love in spite of sin, marching on to victory.

THE USA TODAY

On one hand sits our meek generosity
To our enemy and foreign lands.
On the other hand, not so generous to
The devastation in our country and our land.

Who do you see helping each other,
The states and their people hour by hour?
Where are those we put in power?

Like micromanagers, they ignore our pleas.
And we can't see the forest for the trees.

Games they play against each other,
Which side wins what today for those in power.

Oblivious to the needs and desires of others,
They spend our money on frivolous things,
Spreading o'er the land like gossamer wings.

Still not satisfied, they raise our debt,
Then throw or give it away, to our regret.

Still we grumble and groan
And do nothing to save our way of life or home.

We send our servicepeople into harm's way
For someone else's plight today.

We find ourselves invaded, robbed, beaten, and killed
By invaders and the jobless in desperate need.
Open your eyes, or we may not succeed.

This Is My Story

Chorus:

This is my story.
This is my song.
Loving my Jesus,
All the day long.

Verse 1:

Clothed in His armor,
Holding His sword.
Following Jesus,
My Savior and Lord.

Chorus:

This is my story.
This is my song.
Loving my Jesus,
All the day long.

Verse 2:

Through danger and strife,
I follow His way.
Wherever He leads,
Pressing each day.

Chorus: (twice)

This is my story.
This is my song.
Loving my Jesus,
All the day long.

THIS LAND

Last night I had a dream so grand
That everything was wonderful in this land.
That neighbors walked hand-in-hand.
That prosperity was, oh, so grand.
That the Holy Spirit influenced this land,
Lifting us up with a strong and loving hand.

Then I awoke to find
All my dreams were left behind.

Who is my neighbor anyway?
Will they talk to me or have anything to say?
Or will they scurry past my door and fade away?
Maybe we'll meet another way or another day.
And this is all I have to say.

Time to change and pray.
Tomorrow is another day.
If we do it together this way,
We can look forward to happy days
With the USA, the only way.

Also published in *American Poet,* vol. 2, Eber & Wein Publishing, 2016, page 121.

TIMES OF REFRESHING

Have you ever noticed when you are in sin
Mountains of problems suddenly come pouring in?
You can whine and cry, blaming another,
Dumping hard life on a sister or brother.

Everyone seems to do better than you.
But I have a solution for just what to do.
Repent of your sins to the Lord.
Forgive your brother with love, not a sword.

Let them see the presence of the Spirit in you,
That living the Word will bring rewards anew.
Life will be tolerable when you do,
And joining the Lord's work will see you through.

Inspiration from
Acts 3:11–20.

TITHE AND MORE

Bought a special car at long last.
Just my speed, super-fast.
And got my mate this big, nice house,
My status to arouse.

We could not go to church in unfashionable clothes,
So yet these expenses had arose.
The children, too, needed all the best,
And money was put to the test.

I thank You, Lord, for all of this.
But since my budget is amiss,
I promise to get spending under control.
Then I'll be able to tithe where now it's just a great big hole.

Inspiration from
Romans 12:3–8.

TOMORROW

Have you ever dreamed you could fly
Or spread yourself in space and sky?

Or dreamed the world was oh, so bright
Because things evolved for you just right?

Well, nothing will compare to what you'll see
When with the Lord you will finally be.

Nothing will compare to who you are
When you become God's heavenly bright and shining star.

Tomorrow's Promise

Lead me, oh Lord, and I will follow.
All that was Abraham's will be mine tomorrow.
To be born again begins my journey.
Receiving the Holy Spirit inside of me,
His plan emerging for me to see.

Together we tread the earth.
Through trials and tribulations, we work,
Doing on earth what Jesus began.

For tomorrow will bring the Promised Land.
This I give my total love and devotion
Without reservation or any preconceived notion.

TOO MUCH MAKES
TOO LITTLE

Anyone can eat too much,
And anyone can take too many drinks
If you focus on this world and all its faults and kinks.

Anyone can lust after the things the world unfolds.
But none can pray enough
Or follow what the Bible holds.

Those not born again will always go along,
But Christians let our Holy Spirit
Sing to us a truly loving song.

It brings our ways into focus
On our Abba Father throughout the day.
Then before you know it, thoughts of evil have all passed away.

Inspiration from
Ephesians 5:17–18.

TRANSFORMED

Once evil filled my mind.
But being born again caused me
To walk a different line.

Surrounded by a world of sin,
One could not let temptations of the devil in.
The Holy Spirit now lies inside,
And He must be my only guide.

He'll hold me close and help me grow.
He'll teach me all I need to know.

This is my cross to bear.
Not to conform to the world
But to encourage the world to see
The godly side of me.

Inspiration from
Romans 12:1–2.

TROUBLED WATERS

Everyone wants to give advice.
But whatever it may be
Could be as bad as a storm at sea.

A servant of God is the one to seek,
Who depicts God's Word from week to week.

Inspiration from
Acts 27:3–12.

TRUE LOVE

When two people love each other,
Any mountain can be climbed.
For each focuses on the other
And true love they will find.

So it goes with the Lord,
When you focus on Him
And He on you
To bring a beautiful love affair
That is honest and true.

Inspiration from
Deuteronomy 10:31–44.

TRUST IN HIM

Life is great, and the sun is bright.
Then things turn around overnight.
Like dominoes the great days fall;
Trials and tribulation take it all.

Hard-earned money stretched to the hilt,
Children going astray as parents bear the guilt.
What way to go, which way to turn?
God is watching; will we never learn?

What we face now by our works or the devil's,
Redemption by God will surely follow
If we put Him first and have faith in tomorrow.

TRUST IN THE LORD

When you are happy, the Lord is there.
When you are sad, the Lord is there.

When you work on His behalf, He is there.
And when you hurt, He is there.
He is here, there, and everywhere.

His love will overpower all your ills,
From pain and suffering, the enemy, and even bills.

He'll never forsake you in all you do.
Has He not sent a Comforter to see you through?

Count it all joy that you have Him
For in the end, God's people will always win.

Inspiration from
Acts 23:12–24.

TWO SIDES

There was an old lady who spoke only good.
Everyone in the area knew that she would.

Determined to make her more like them,
They offered this challenge to her, saying,
"Friend, if you see some good in all,
Won't the devil be an exception? It's your call."

After only a short silence she said, "No siree.
The devil does a good job, as you can see."

Here is a lesson you can learn from her.
Love, learn, close the lips, and you'll agree,
That there are two sides you can readily see.
On which side do you want to be?

UNCONDITIONAL LOVE

The parable of the prodigal son
Hasn't changed from happenings today
In every portion, in every way.

Father loves son, but son doesn't care.
His senses are aroused by pleasure in the air,
Taking for granted all that is there.

But don't despair for he'll soon find out
There is nothing there.
If you have exposed him to God and church,
When the worldly forsakes him, he'll end his search.

And what of the others who don't rebel?
Their reward is in heaven and an earthly father as well.
Both love and guide him from birth
To accomplish God's plan here on earth.

WALKING WITH CHRIST

To love one another is to love God.
This is His greatest of all gifts.
To walk in His shadow has equal risks.

Like hunger, rejection, cruelty,
Cold, persecution, and pain.
All of these may be abundant,
Like summer rain.

But listen and hear that when
You grow weary and weak,
He will lift you up, your soul to keep.

You'll walk on water and not feel the fire
If you have faith that God sees your desire.
Nothing that man could do to you
Should take away the Father's work you do.

WALKING WITHOUT FEAR

The devil may lurk like a lion looking for prey,
But you need not fear for the Lord will guide your way.
First, obtain His mercy and grace
Then sing His song, and give Him praise.

What you do may influence many—
Even turn them to Jesus, thus making them ready.
With the Holy Spirit as your guide to lead you through,
There isn't anything you can't do.

Jesus at the helm—
Punishing sin, healing, and a miracle or two—
Will confirm the beauty He can work through you.

We Give Thanks

Pilgrims landed at Plymouth rock
And prayed to God for what they got.
A feast, a harvest of plenty, confidence,
This would be the first of many.

Struggling hard through winter cold,
Through it all remaining strong and bold,
Established for all a freedom grand
In America, the promised land.

Also published in my first book, *Through My Eyes*, AuthorHouse, 2008, page 18.

WE GIVE THANKS TO GOD

Family and friends gather at Thanksgiving,
Goodwill to all in loving and giving.
For all God has given on this earth,
Enhancing our life for all it's worth.

Better yet comes Christmas each year,
Celebrating our Savior with giving and cheer.

Be thankful He came to save us
Without fanfare or fuss,
Born to show the way.
We continue what He started, day by day.

Inspiration from
Acts 28:23–31.

WHAT HAVE WE DONE?

Life is but a fleeting glance.
From beginning to end, a life of chance.
"Me" and "my" seems the order of today,
While "you" slowly fades away.
What did we do along the way?

When tomorrow becomes today and
Today becomes yesterday,
Our brains invent the driverless car.
Yet chaos, death, and destruction
Outweigh by far.

Have all our dreams come true?
What did we actually do?
Have we made our life worthwhile
With an impression on man, woman, and child?

Have we walked with the Lord through this land?
Did we offer love and a helping hand,
Extending His Word as best we can,
Preparing for the Lord and life so grand?

Are we in the days of sorrow?
Will we be here today and gone tomorrow?

Pray, pray, pray.

WHEN IT'S TIME

Those who stand in disbelief
Will face a time of pain and grief.

Yet all can be turned around,
One's life turned upside down.
The way you were will cease to be
As the will of Jesus, you can begin to see.

The choice is yours; you must know
Great things will happen as you grow
If Jesus you will seek to know.

Inspiration from
Acts 8:1–9.

WHEN SIN DIED

God cannot be with sin,
Nor sin with Him.
For us Jesus became sin,
And sin had to die for us to begin.

Before God could receive
Jesus, you, or me, sin had to die.
God did not forsake Jesus
But the sin He became.

Once it was gone,
A new life would dawn.
So it is with us today.
We must continue to push sin away.

To hear from God, Jesus, or the Holy Spirit,
We must ask forgiveness, and let Him hear it.

Inspiration from
Matthew 27:46–56.

WHILE WE WAIT

The precious blood of Jesus,
Who knew no sin,
Through His grace opened up the door
And let us in.

We are redeemed
When confessing our sins
And asking for forgiveness.
So the healing begins.

Pledging our lives to Him
And dying to self
Will open our hearts
To the Holy Spirit for help.

His righteousness through faith,
Maintaining one's existence while we wait,
Knowing He is never early nor late.

Inspiration from
Romans 3:9–12.

WHO ARE YOU?

Who we are, no one knows,
Except from the top of the head
To the all-important toes.

People see what you want them to see
For we are not as transparent as we could be.
Yet no matter how much we hide,
The Lord sees all that lies inside.

We are not an island by our self.
Keeping things inside can affect our health.

Confess your sins, and let them go.
Then only the good is bound to show.
What you reap you'll also sow.
Problems solved each day will help you grow.

Inspiration from
Psalm 51:3;
Galatians 6:3.

WHY ME?

It's a roller-coaster ride.
First, life is good, including my pride.
Then everything goes wrong,
And my life becomes a sad song.

Why did God do this to me?
He didn't! Now I see.
He saved me from my sin
And took me to Him all over again.

Remember, pride comes before the fall.
Grow close to God again or lose it all.

Your Father watches over you,
And He will do what He must do
To save the likes of me and you.

Inspiration from
1 Timothy 6:6–10.

WISDOM

God made you what you are
To be a bright and shining star.
Best is the inner beauty by far.

Remember God made all things.
Do not worry about what life brings
For God is in control.

Let the Holy Spirit be your guide.
Prayer and supplication are on your side.
And do not try to control circumstance and man.
But offer, when asked, a guiding hand.

Inspiration from
Isaiah 26:3;
Philippians 4:7.

Wisdom of Solomon

Just how do we know the difference between
Wisdom and folly, prosperity over poverty,
Good versus evil, or life over death?

Friend over enemy, truth or a lie?
To whom we say hello and to whom we say goodbye?
How do we know?
By the Holy Spirit, who tells us so.

Is not He a part of the Trinity?
Love the Lord, and you will see
God works through Jesus, and He through
the Holy Ghost, then onto you and me.
As Jesus revealed, this is the way it will be.

WISDOM TO DISCERN

Discernment in right and wrong,
Good and evil, is not in a book or how you look.
It comes from others, like fathers and mothers
And teachers, friends, sisters, and brothers.

Yes, wisdom is to learn from another,
Seeing what is good and what is not.
How they make corrections with what they've got.

Age has wisdom to unfold.
A wisdom more precious than gold.
But the biggest leader of all we do
Comes from the Holy Spirit's influence on you.

Are you listening? Will you see
All the plans He has for you and me?

Inspiration from
Philippians 1:9–10;
Hebrews 5:14.

WITHOUT FEAR

You think the world is falling apart,
And all of this breaks your heart.
Do not fear; the Lord is here.

Good called evil and evil called good
As related in the Bible, now understood.
You do your part, and I'll do mine.
And those who do, God won't leave behind.

You may be persecuted here,
But find consolation in knowing God is near.
And in the end, you'll be with the King of men.

You Can't Steal My Joy

You can knock me down.
You can steel my car.
You can take my job,
And sit on my pride.
But you can't steal my joy
For that comes from the Lord.

You can slander my name.
You can take my fame.
You can throw stones.
You can take my home.
But you can't steal my joy
For that comes from the Lord.

You can make me ill.
You can sway my friends.
You can shatter my dreams.
You can do anything.
But you can't steal my joy
For that comes from the Lord.

Also published in my first book, *Through My Eyes,* AuthorHouse, 2008, page 4.

YOUR CHOICE

There are two punishments for every crime,
Two sets of rules on earthly time.
One set made by God and the other by man.
Both to follow as best you can.

Love is the way to manage it all.
Love picks you up when you fall.
Love your enemies but don't participate.
Pray for their souls and mourn their fate.

For God has planned your destiny,
And the Holy Spirit guides you for all to see.
Love is more rewarding than evil
For it brings comfort and peace to its people.

Inspiration from
Romans 12:18;
Hebrews 12:14.

Your Mentor's Book

Your Bible is your guide,
With parables everywhere inside,
Teaching you right from wrong
And how He wants you to move along.

It won't stop the perils you face
But show how to react with style and grace.
Reading the Bible brings you closer to God
And directs the path on which you trod.

Holding the hand of the Lord
Affords one protection and use of His sword.
So praise and seek Him constantly
And know the rewards are bound to be.

Inspiration from
Psalm 1:1–6.

Printed in the United States
By Bookmasters